The Face of Urbanization and Urban Poverty in Bangladesh

Pranab Kumar Panday

The Face of Urbanization and Urban Poverty in Bangladesh

Explaining the Slum Development Initiatives in the light of Global Experiences

palgrave
macmillan

Pranab Kumar Panday
Department of Public Administration
University of Rajshahi
Rajshahi, Bangladesh

ISBN 978-981-15-3331-0 ISBN 978-981-15-3332-7 (eBook)
https://doi.org/10.1007/978-981-15-3332-7

This Palgrave Macmillan imprint is published by the registered company Springer Nature Singapore Pte Ltd.
The registered company address is: 152 Beach Road, #21-01/04 Gateway East, Singapore 189721, Singapore

Preface

Modernization, along with urbanization, is seen as a sign of growth and economic progress. The rapid growth of urbanization has affected people in different parts of the globe. The process of Urbanization, a relatively new phenomenon in developing countries, was already complete in the industrialized countries in the last century. This hasty growth of urbanization in the developing countries, doing in less than a lifetime what took centuries elsewhere, has outpaced economic growth and modernization in some countries. Like other parts of the world, South Asian countries in general, and Bangladesh in particular, have been undergoing rapid urbanization, which is making it difficult for the Government to maintain social and economic integration.

Urbanization has a strong relationship with poverty and migration. Poverty is the main push factor that compels large numbers of people in different parts of developing countries to migrate to urban areas in search of jobs. Also, modern amenities of life, in the form of better working opportunities, better infrastructure, better education and health facilities and opportunities for enjoyment are luring rural people to migrate to cities. Once these people arrive in cities they find themselves in a strange place: they have no social network; modes and methods of transport are strange to them; everything costs money and a lot of it; they start at the bottom of the heap and their promised comfort and wealth usually does not exist. They leave the village poor and actually, in many cases, become poorer in the cities. They lived in huts in the village, with no water or electricity, which was normal for everyone. But when they have to live in a hut in the city, with no water or electricity, where many people have modern toilets and the latest computers and appliances, they feel that they have lost everything. Arriving with nothing, they cannot buy land or a house that would give them tenure and, in the developing countries, land tenure is the first requirement for services like electricity, water and sanitation that are provided by the municipal bodies. Migration from village Hell to urban Heaven has become migration from peaceful village to dangerous, deprived and desperate slums.

Many writers have studied the effects of hasty urbanization in the developing world. Jones (2003) used three transitions to discuss contemporary research and policy on urbanization. The hasty urbanization that the developing countries have been experiencing is the first transition. It has been predicted by many international organizations and researchers that 80% of the world's population would live in urban areas by 2025 (Mooya and Chris 2007). This would make the systematic development efforts of urban areas problematic due to the relentless growth of informal settlements (Durand-Lasserve and Royston 2002).

Jones (2003) identified poverty as the second transition among the effects of urbanization. Notably, the growth rate of urban poverty in developing countries is about the same as the growth rate in urbanization. The 2018 revised version of World's Urbanization Prospects shows that 41% people of lower-middle-income countries were living in urban areas in 2018 while the ratio was 32% in lower-income countries. The report also projected that these percentages would be on average 59% and 50%, respectively, in 2050 (United Nations 2019).

Jones' (2003) third transition among the effects of urbanization was property rights. This is what would turn desperate squatters into settled residents. Although we are yet to finalize a clear definition of what constitutes "urban" in Bangladesh, we are experiencing an extremely high growth rate of urbanization. Due to the migration of increasingly more people from rural areas to cities, the country has become one of the most hurriedly urbanized countries in Asia. This hasty urbanization casts mammoth burdens on cities by aggravating and extending urban poverty. Accordingly, a growing number of the urban poor, without any access to amenities and without any land rights, are living in substandard slums.

Over the years, these desperate urban poor are becoming a serious challenge to the cities, especially on the issue of housing. There are, increasingly, two classes of housing in the urban areas of developing countries:

state-of-the-art houses for the successful and unserved slums for everyone else. Thus, the issues of urbanization, urban poverty and slum development are closely related.

The substandard lifestyle and suffering of the people of the slums have influenced Governments and other actors to look for strategies through which urban misery can be alleviated. In this connection, the strategy of slum upgrading has been development, as alternatives like relocation of slum dwellers is quite difficult for most countries. Considering the importance of slum upgrading, Governments, as well as international organizations and NGOs, have been working on implementing this policy. Yet it is very difficult to conclude that slum-upgrading initiatives have been successful. In this book, a few slum-upgrading examples that were successful have been presented as "best practice" models. As in other developing countries, several slum-upgrading initiatives have also been implemented in Bangladesh.

This book focuses on the relationship of urbanization, urban poverty and slum development initiatives. Both global and Bangladeshi case studies are considered. The book takes up initiative to discuss the theoretical linkages among urbanization, urban poverty and slum development; the relationship between slum formation and slum upgradation initiatives; the global strategies needed to address the issue of urban slum development; and the major challenges facing slum-upgrading initiatives in Bangladesh and their possible solutions. Very few efforts have been made to present an all-inclusive analysis of the urbanization, urban poverty and slum-upgrading initiatives in Bangladesh. No other book has tried to do this. Therefore, this book intends to fill the existing gaps by considering these issues as the whole that they are.

Rajshahi, Bangladesh — Pranab Kumar Panday

References

Durand-Lasserve, A., & Royston, L. (2002). *Holding their ground: Secure land tenure for the urban poor in developing countries*. London: Earthscan.

Jones, G. A. (Ed.). (2003). *Urban land markets in transition*. CD ROM. Cambridge, MA: Lincoln Institute of Land Policy.

Mooya, M. M., & Chris E. C. (2007). Informal urban property markets and poverty alleviation: A conceptual framework. *Urban Studies, 44*(1), 147–165.

United Nations. (2019). *World urbanization prospects: The 2018 revision*. New York: Department of Economic and Social Affairs (Population Department).

Contents

Abbreviations

ADB	Asian Development Bank
ADP	Annual Development Program
ANC	African National Congress
ASARC	Australia South Asia Research Centre
ASEH	Advancing Sustainable Environmental Health
BDTK	Bangladesh Taka
BIP	Basti Improvement Program
BOSC	Bastee Basheer Odhikar Surakha Committees
BRAC	Bangladesh Rural Advancement Committee
BRICS	Brazil, Russia, India, China and South Africa
BUILD	Building Union Infrastructure for Local Development
BURT	Bangladesh Urban Round Table
CARE	Cooperative for American Relief Everywhere
CDD	Community Driven Development
CDF	Community Development Fund
CEPAL	Economic Commission for Latin America
CKIP	Comprehensive Kampung Improvement program
CODI	Community Organizations Development Institute
CSG	Community Self-help Group
CTLS	Community-Led Total Sanitation Program
CUDP	Calcutta Urban Development Program
CUP	Coalition for the Urban Poor
CUS	Centre for Urban Studies
DCC	Dhaka City Corporation
DFID	Department for International Development

DMP	Disaster Management Program
DPRU	Development Policy Research Units
DSK	Sushtha Shasthya Kendra
DWASA	Dhaka Water Supply and Sewerage Authority
ECLA	Eugene Comprehensive Lands Assessment
EGM	Extraordinary General Meeting
ESCAP	United Nations Economic and Social Commission for Asia and the Pacific
FFP	Food for Peace
FGI	Fertile Grounds Initiative
FPP	Flood Proofing Project
GB	Government of Bangladesh
GDP	Gross Domestic Program
GIS	Geographic Information System
GIZ	German Society for International Cooperation
GNP	Gross National Product
GOB	Government of Bangladesh
GPI	Gap Poverty Index
GTZ	German Technical Cooperation Agency
HDRC	Human Development Research Centre
HIES	Household Income and Expenditure Survey
HPI	Headcount Poverty Indices
HUDCO	Housing and Urban Development Cooperation
ICSECR	International Covenant on Economic, Social and Cultural Rights
IDS	Institute of Development Studies
IFSP	Fourth Integrated Food Security Program
IGA	Income Generating Activities
IGES	Institute for Global Environmental Strategies
IIED	International Institute for Environment and Development
IOM	International Organization for Migration
JOWICE	Journal of Women in Colleges of Education
KDB	Kampung Development Board
KIP	Comprehensive Kampung Improvement
LCG	Local Consultative Group
LGC	Local Government Code
LGD	Local Government Division
LGED	Local Government Engineering Department
LOSAUK	Lokenattya O Sanskritik Unnayan Kendro
LPS	Low Performing State
LPUPAP	Local Partnership for Urban Poverty Reduction Project
MDG	Millennium Development Goals
MEC	Multi Economic-based Cooperation

NA	Not Applicable
NEC	National Economic Council
NGO	Nongovernmental Organization
NSAPR	National Strategy for Accelerated Poverty Reduction
NSDP	National Slum Development Program
NY	New York
OD	Community-led total sanitation
PAF	Poverty Alleviation Fund
PNGO	Palestinian Nongovernmental Organization
PRSP	Poverty Reduction Strategy Paper
PSF	People's Survival Fund
PSTC	Population Services and Training Centre
RICS	Royal Institute of Chartered Surveyors
SC	Supervision Council
SHAHAR	Supporting Household Activities for Hygiene, Assets and Revenue
SIP	Slum Improvement Project
SPARC	Society for the Promotion of Areas Resource Centres
SRA	Slum Rehabilitation Authority
STWSSSP	Secondary Towns Water Supply and Sanitation Sector Project
STWSSSP	Small Towns Water Supply and Sanitation Sector Project
UBSDP	Urban basic Service delivery Project
UCDO	Urban Community Development Organization
UCLG	United Cities and Local Governments
UK	United Kingdom
UN	United Nations
UNAPCAEM	Comprehensive Review of the Work of the United Nations Asian and Pacific Centre for Agricultural Engineering and Machinery
UNCEDAW	Convention on the Elimination of all Forms of Discrimination against Women
UNCHS	United Nations Centre for Human Settlements
UNCRC	United National Child Rights Convention
UN-DESA	United Nations Department of Economic and Social Affairs
UNDP	United Nations Development Program
UNFP	United Nations Population Fund
UN-HABITAT	United Nations Human Settlements Program
UNICEF	United Nations Children's Emergency Fund
UNUWIDER	United Nations University World Institute for Development Economics Research
UP	Union Parishad
UPL	University Press Limited

UPPRP	Urban Partnerships for Poverty Reduction Project
UPWARD	Users' Perspectives With Agricultural Research and Development
USA	United States of America
VAMBAY	Valmiki Ambedkar Awas Yojana
VERC	Village Education Resource Centre
WATSAN	Water and Sanitation
WB	World Bank
WEDC	Water Engineering and Development Centre
WHO	World Health Organization
WSUP	Water and Sanitation for the Urban Poor

List of Tables

CHAPTER 1

Introduction

Introduction

Urbanization is an important manifestation of modernization. Modernization has been considered to be a sign of growth and economic progress. The whole world has been affected by the growth of urbanization. Although the process of urbanization is almost complete in rich industrialized countries, it is a recent phenomenon in the context of developing countries. Thus, developing countries are experiencing urbanization at such a rapid pace that it exceeds their economic growth and their ability to finance it. Like other developed countries, South Asian countries in general, and Bangladesh in particular, have been undergoing a rapid growth in urbanization. Urbanization has been so rapid in these countries that it makes it difficult for the government to maintain social and economic integration and provide for all the impoverished newcomers to the cities.

Since the issue of urbanization has great implications for both developed and developing countries, Jones (2003) discusses the contemporary research and policy formulation on this issue, identifying a number of transitions in the process. The first transition, especially in developing countries, is excessively rapid—we say "hasty"—urbanization. The rate of urbanization is so fast in these countries that many have estimated that 80% of the population of these countries will be living in urban areas by 2025 (Mooya and Chris 2007). Such an excessive speed of urbanization will impel the growth of informal settlements. Historically, these two

P. K. Panday, *The Face of Urbanization and Urban Poverty in Bangladesh*, https://doi.org/10.1007/978-981-15-3332-7_1

concepts—rapid urbanization and the growth of informal settlements—have a close relationship (Durand-Lasserve and Royston 2002).

Poverty, according to Jones (2003), is the second transition. The inhabitants of the informal settlements that spring up in the first transition are mostly, desperately poor. They arrive with nothing and, at least for a long time, have almost nothing. As a result, we see that the rate of increase in urban poverty is far higher than that in rural poverty. The rapid growth in the numbers of the urban poor has made international organizations, like the Department of International Development, express their concern in 2003. They projected that if urban population growth persists at the current rate, more than 67% of the poor in Latin America, East and Central Europe, and Central Asia will be living in urban areas by 2025. They also predicted that more than one-third, up to as many as half, of the poor in Africa and Asia will be living in urban areas by that year.

Property rights is the third transition, according to Jones (2003). This develops as a political, economic and social issue directly from the repopulation of most urban areas with poor, desperate, rural migrants in Jones' (2003) transitions 1 and 2. The unholy trinity of Urbanization, Poverty and Slums, are closely related and have thus gained paramount importance as the issue of discussion on development in academic and development fields.

Bangladesh, too, has been experiencing the sort of "hasty" urbanization and resultant problems of urban poverty and slumification of cities described earlier. Continuous and relentless movement of people from rural areas to cities in larger numbers has branded Bangladesh as one of the most urbanized countries in Asia. Yet, while this process occurred in Europe over a period of 300 years, it has, as in most other developing countries, happened in Bangladesh in a single generation. The rapid urbanization is creating enormous pressure on cities, thus, aggravating urban poverty. The increasing numbers of the urban poor are posing a serious challenge to the cities in terms of providing an acceptable quality of housing (Panday 2017). There are, increasingly, two classes of housing in the urban areas of Bangladesh, as in other developing countries: state-of-the-art houses for the successful and poorly serviced slums for everyone else. Thus, the issues of urbanization, urban poverty and slum development are closely related.

In the existing literature, there is no comprehensive work that has shed light on the issues of urbanization, urban poverty and slum development in Bangladesh. Thus, intending to fill this gap, this book discusses these three concepts in a single frame. The book aims to provide a clear understanding of the relationship among these interrelated issues in Bangladesh: (1) what is the theoretical linkage between urbanization, urban poverty and slum development; (2) what is the relationship between slum formation and slum upgrading initiatives; (3) how has the issue of urban slum development has been addressed globally; (4) what are the major urban slum-upgrading practices in Bangladesh and (5) what are the major challenges for slum development initiatives in Bangladesh and how can they be resolved? The book is mainly based on the analysis of secondary materials.

Urbanization, Urban Poverty and Slum Development: An Analysis of Their Interrelationship in Bangladesh

As stated earlier, urbanization is one of the most talked-about development issues in the modern development discourse. One of the most serious manifestations of urbanization is the rapid increase of urban poverty in these countries. On the other hand, urban growth, or urbanization, and urban poverty have proliferated with the growth of slums and squatter settlements in most developing countries. The enormity of the issue is not a new phenomenon in development literature.

For instance, UN-HABITAT (2003a), in its global slum assessment report, mentioned that 32% of the world's population (which was around 924 million in 2003) was living in slums, while in developing countries, 43% was living in slums. At least, the awareness of the problem dates back to the beginning of this century.

Living conditions in these slums are awful and they also damage the environment. Common descriptions of slums include lack of water supply, unhygienic sanitation facilities, congested and ramshackle habitation, perilous location and anxiety over tenure, among other kinds of social and economic deprivation. The proliferation of substandard living conditions gave rise to Target 11 of the Millennium Development Goals (MDGs) that made a commitment to substantially upgrade living conditions for the 100 million people who, it was estimated, would be living in slums by the year 2020 (UN-HABITAT 2003b).

McGranahan and Martine (2014) stated that the hasty growth of the slum communities, drawing poor people in from the rural areas, has made urban poverty a serious challenge for many of the developing societies.

Thus, migration-induced urban poverty has manifested in inadequate and irregular incomes, which define urban poverty in most developing countries. The problem is that the urban economy is informal and irregular, while the costs of living of the poor who live and work in it are fixed and rising. Low-income people, trying to live "the city life" buy necessities at the same prices as do the rich, but do not have equivalent or regular incomes.

Yet income cannot be considered the only indicator of urban poverty. Housing conditions, even for slum dwellers who earn middle-class incomes, but not enough to leave the slums, also need to be considered. This is because, increasingly in developing countries, cities are becoming places of modern state-of-the-art accommodation surrounded by teeming slums. Thus, a slum dweller who improves his or her income has nowhere to go unless he or she can jump the middle class into true wealth. More than a billion urban people are compelled to stay in overcrowded hovels with no legal rights to the land on which they sleep. Worse, the people living in these illegal hovels do not get access to public services in the form of roads, drainage, potable water and sewerage health, education, police or emergency services (Tacoli 2017). Along with their other sufferings, slum dwellers can never feel secure because they are liable to attack by criminals, landlords and the local or central government that wants to clear the slums (Satterthwaite 2003).

People staying in these illegal houses also have to contend with the threat of crime, violence and insecurity, lack of access to credit and absence of voting rights. Access to these non-income facilities requires legal status with official land tenure documents to prove it, which these people do not have. Thus, they pay disproportionate costs to buy community services like water, sewage disposal, schooling and health care (Tacoli 2017).

Another dimension of urban poverty and slum settlement is the gender dimension of the impact of inadequate community services. Most slum women are too busy doing household activities and providing care to children and elders at home to develop careers. They are also affected by health-related problems due to pollution and lack of health care. They do not find a safe place to take care of their children or to prepare food for family members. Whenever they want to get involved in paid jobs, the scope is very limited: low pay for long hours as household helpers is available to them (Degaga 2010).

The issue of the impact of substandard, illegal housing on the security of urban food and nutrition has been one of the least-researched areas in development literature. While good food is available in the urban markets, people living in poor settlements cannot afford them. In slums, there is little space to grow fruits and vegetables, let alone keep animals. This issue needs to be considered in both its food and non-food aspects (Tacoli et al. 2013).

Like other developing countries of the world, Bangladesh has seen a rapid growth in urbanization. While the problem may cease to grow so rapidly in future, the UN has projected that the country will have 86.5 million people in cities by 2030 (UN-HABITAT 2013). If the growth continues at the same rate, the urban share of the total population would exceed the 50% mark by 2040 and 60% by the year 2050. At that point, the number of people in urban areas in 2050 would be more than 100 million (Islam 2012).

Urban poverty, as stated earlier, is a manifestation of the hasty urbanization of the country. Rural people flood the underserviced cities and the State sector of developing countries does not have the resources to provide the housing and other normal amenities they need. Thus, they are condemned to a substandard life without basic services (Saleh and Khan 2017).

How can poor countries deal with hasty urbanization and the poverty it creates? One easy way to deal with the issue is to ensure availability of resources that will respond to and support urban or local authorities, emphasizing on the capabilities of inhabitants, ensuring the privileges of entire populations to elementary facilities, ensuring rule of law and establishing responsible organizations. We cannot ignore the fact that poor people are subjected to different types of deprivation in the form of insufficient consumption of food, scarce resources, problems relating to the condition of health of people living in substandard houses, the fight for safer water and improved sanitation, the complications in receiving appropriate care of health and sending children to school, and the extended working hours in unsafe situations. What they need are (1) resources and (2) organization. Yet most developing countries have neither. Given that their private sector resources are also inadequate and can be tapped nor taxed, they need help from developed countries, international investors or international organizations to address these problems. The absence of land tenure rights has made slum dwellers vulnerable. The Government of Bangladesh has acknowledged the importance of the issue of slum development and has incorporated it in its action under Sustainable Development Goal 11 ("make cities and human settlements inclusive, safe, resilient and sustainable"). Target 11 of the MDG was also similar. By designing a "New Urban Agenda" in line with the guidelines of the UN-Habitat III Cities Conference, held in Quito, Ecuador on 20 October 2016, the Government of Bangladesh intends to guide all urban development actors, including policy-makers, civil society, development funders and international organizations to reach the goal of having safe housing as a human right of the slum dwellers. This would be transformative social change. In addition to this, the Government of Bangladesh has also enacted a National Housing Policy, to guarantee the housing rights of every citizen (Saleh and Khan 2017). Thus, the issue of slum upgrading has become a policy agenda of the Government as well as of local and international organizations.

Land Tenure Rights of Slum Dwellers in Bangladesh

The Constitution of Bangladesh, in Article 15 (1), affirms that "It shall be a fundamental responsibility of the state to .... provide basic necessities of life, including food, clothing, shelter, education and medical care". Moreover, Articles 31 and 32 also guarantee the fundamental rights of the citizens to protection and life in accordance with law (The Constitution of Bangladesh 2016). In addition to the Constitutional guarantees, the National Housing Policy, 1993, considered a milestone in the field of ensuring people's rights to housing, set out goals of slum improvement while protecting the rights of slum dwellers not to be evicted without better alternative housing (Islam 2004). The 1999 National Housing Policy Amendments emphasized the facilitative role of the private sector's development of housing for all, including the poor. Moreover, the Government of Bangladesh has ratified a number of international agreements or treaties, including the International Covenant on Economic, Social and Cultural Rights (ICSECR), the UN Convention on the Elimination of all Forms of Discrimination against Women (UNCEDAW), and the UN Child Rights Convention (UNCRC), that also speak of the rights of shelter for all.

To achieve shelter for all requires confronting the issue of security of tenure for slum dwellers. Security without ownership is a pipedream. The system of land tenure in Bangladesh has a very complex history and is now quite insecure and unsettled. In many cases, it is not quite certain who owns slum land. The majority of the urban poor and extremely poor in Bangladesh informally occupy their homes with no real legal right to do so.

In Bangladesh, 90% of the urban poor do not have tenure rights. They are squatting on State land or private property. At least 20 types of informal tenure arrangements exist for the poor, all illegal (Mostafa n.d.). In many cases, slums are considered transit places for people who believe that they are on the road from the village to a better life. Lack of legal tenure rights makes these people feel constantly insecure, in fear of dispossession by the true landowner or the State (Jayarantne 2009). Tables 1.1 and 1.2 show the different urban land tenure types in Bangladesh as found by three independent studies.

Table 1.1 Urban land tenure types in Bangladesh

Study-1 (Islam et al. 2007)	*Study-2 (Shafi and Payne 2007)*	*Study-3 (UNDP 2006)*
1 Nonformal, de facto tenure	1. Street dwellers	1. Land over which occupants claim "ownership"
2. Private freehold	2. Tenant bed rental (Mess housing)	2. Land on which occupants have a lease for varying lengths of time
3. Government of *khas* land	3. Tenant room rental	3. Permission to stay and use the land
4. Public leasehold	4. Squatter tenant	4. Rental agreements
5. Private leasehold	5. Squatter	5. Informally occupied land
6. Apartment tenure	6. Tenant—on registered and subdivided land	
7. Community ownership	7. Owner—on unregistered and subdivided land	
8. Cooperative Ownership	8. Legal tenant no contract	
9. Wakf (charitable/ religious land)	9. Legal tenant with contract	
10. Abandoned property	10. Tied tenant	
11. The nonresident vested property	11. Leaseholder	
	12. Cooperative member	
	13. Communal owner	
	14. The individual owner	

Source: Adapted from Mostafa (n.d.: 7). and Jayarantne, K. A. (2009)

Table 1.2 Types of informal and formal tenure

Types of informal tenure		*Types of informal tenure*	
1. Street dwellers:	Persons or families living on pavements or the side of the streets. Practically without a roof over their head. The duration can vary from days to months.	9. Legal tenant with contract:	A tenant renting legally developed a land/house with a legal contract. Normally a yearly contract.
2. Tenant, bed rental (Mess housing):	People living by renting bed space as in hostels/ dormitories. Not very common and exists only in major cities, around city centres and close to industrial establishments. This type is commonly known as a 'mess' type of accommodation.	10. Tied Tenant:	A tenant who occupies residential quarters as an employee of the government, semi-government and private commercial and industrial organizations. Tenure security is tied to retaining employment.
3. Tenant room rental:	Renting rooms with shared facilities. Accommodation is temporary by nature. May occur on public or private land and public or private housing.	11. Leaseholder:	Possession of land/house under a lease agreement with the landowner (public or private).
4. Squatter tenant:	Tenants in squatter built houses generally on public land.	12. Cooperative member:	Enjoys land and housing as a member of a registered cooperative society.
5. Squatter:	Person or family living on land belonging to another, usually in the self-constructed house generally on public land.	13. Communal owner:	Owners who belong to a group and live in one area and enjoy community welfare and mutual support.
6. Tenant—on unregistered and subdivided land:	Rental accommodation in housing built on land that has been subdivided and purchased but not registered.	14. Individual owner:	Enjoy land/housing legally and have access to the rights of selling/transfer or development of the property.
7. Owner—on unregistered and subdivided land:	Legal owners of unregistered land with the building which may be unauthorized, generally known as illegal subdivision.		
8. Legal tenant no contract:	A tenant living in legal housing under a verbal agreement.		

Source: Adapted from Mostafa (n.d.: 8)

Legal land tenure opens access to basic services like infrastructure, employment and financial institutions. Land tenure security also acts as a social capital that helps the households to enjoy a significant level of social status and financial security, as the land title is one of the low-income community's "portfolio of assets" (Moser 2007) and allows owners to borrow from banks for investment.

For instance, one of the greatest challenges of the people living in slums is the lack of safe drinking water and other water supply for cleaning and hygiene. This problem has been intensified due to the absence of municipal and private water and sanitation services in slum settlements. The main problem is that the law requires those who seek connection to local government water services to show ownership of the relevant land. Such provision of the law is contradictory to the basic principles of the State policies that require the government to deliver sufficient services to citizens, such as water and sanitation. Of course, the Government explains that they do not want to change the law to encourage squatting by providing services to squatters. Moreover, the Government fears that people who do not own the land can never pay for the water as connection is a costly process. Yet the slum dwellers pay far more to access the water by the bucket as they would pay for the pipe, calculated on a per liter basis (Retrieved from https://www.ucl.ac.uk/dpu-projects/drivers_urb_change/urb_infrastructure/pdf_land%20tenure/WaterAid_Land_Tenure.pdf, accessed on 24/12/2017).

Importance of the Book

Despite Constitutional guarantees, the housing rights of a large portion of people living in slums have not been safeguarded. One of the prime reasons is urban poverty, which is one of the manifestations of rapid urbanization. Thus, the issue of slum development is an important agenda for the development organizations and the Government of Bangladesh.

In order to deal with the issue of slum improvement, different programs in the name of slum clearance and slum resettlement were implemented by governments of different countries and international donor organizations. However, considering the importance of the issue, these programs have been replaced by slum upgrading or development. Demolishing and rebuilding the slums proved to be beyond the financial capacity of the developing countries' governments, as well as being extremely disrupting to the lives of slum dwellers (World Bank 2006). As compared to the failure of most slum resettlement programs, slum upgrading attained a greater amount of success in different countries, including Thailand, Indonesia, Sri Lanka, Pakistan, and in some places in India.

Thus, in light of these success stories, slum-upgrading initiatives were also introduced in Bangladesh. Successful factors have included fulfillment of the project objectives, community participation, availability of resources, and approaches of the State agencies (Khan 2007).

It is important to mention here that there are numerous slum upgradations or development or improvement programs that have been implemented in different parts of the world. Among those, some of them have attained tremendous success while others have failed to attain the desired level of success. Along with other countries, the Government of Bangladesh, along with different international donor organizations, with the assistance of national organizations, has been implementing various programs intending to ensure positive development in the living standards of people in the slums. Now a pertinent question is whether the modalities of different slum upgrading have succeeded or failed in different developing countries. This book asks the following questions: to what extent are urbanization, urban poverty and slums interrelated in Bangladesh; are slum-upgrading programs that are being implemented in Bangladesh different to programs that are being implemented elsewhere; and what are the best practices in slum development initiatives and how we could learn lessons from them to revamp our programs in this regard?

This book attempts to provide a comprehensive discussion on the theoretical and practical interrelationship of urbanization, urban poverty and slum development initiatives that are being implemented globally and in Bangladesh. The book will help to identify best practices of urban slum development initiatives from the global perspective and how those can be included in slum development initiatives in Bangladesh.

This book intends to fill current gaps in the literature through the accumulation of new knowledge on urbanization, urban poverty and slum development in South Asia in general and Bangladesh in particular. One of the notable gaps is that there is hardly any book that has considered urban poverty and slum development initiatives globally and in a country-specific context in a single frame. Thus, it is expected that the book will identify different dimensions of urban poverty, best practices of slum development initiatives, and challenges of the implementation of these programs. Based on the findings, the Government and different development partners will be able to redesign their implementation strategies with regard to reducing urban poverty and to better improve the living conditions of slum dwellers.

Most importantly, the book will help readers comprehend the variety and advantages of different slum development initiatives in a global perspective. This would allow the readers to make a comparison of the operating procedures of different programs.

The book will first operationalize the concept of best practices and, based on these criteria, will identify a number of best practices of the slum improvement initiatives. With an intention to assist policy-makers and development practitioners to identify their missing links, and receive feedback on the lessons learnt by those best practices. Accordingly, they would be placed in a better position to redesign their existing programs or future initiatives. Thus, we can learn the lessons of the past and make better choices for the future. Most importantly, it is expected that the book will deliver a comprehensive scrutiny of the issue of urbanization, urban poverty and slum development initiatives from a global and a Bangladesh perspective.

Organization of the Book

Chapter 1: Introduction

Almost all developing countries are confronted with "hasty" urbanization, resulting in the growth of urban poverty. As a consequence of urbanization, millions of people are moving from rural to urban areas in the hope of living a better life. Once they arrive in the cities, they begin to live a life worse than before. They raise their incomes somewhat, if they are lucky, but also increase their costs beyond their capacity to pay. Even problems solved simply in the village, like food, housing and sanitation, become unending crises. Thus, they are compelled to live in slums where they do not get access to basic services. This chapter presents the underlying dilemma of the rural migrant to the slum in Bangladesh. It also introduces the main objectives and issues in the book. The relationship among urbanization, urban poverty and slum development is introduced and set out in stark reality. There is a modest attempt to discuss the Constitutional guarantees concerning housing rights.

Chapter 2: Theoretical Debates on Urbanization and Urban Poverty

This chapter sheds light on the detailed theoretical debate on the issue of urbanization and urban poverty. In the first half of the chapter, an attempt has been made to discuss the meaning of concepts like urban, urbanism, urbanized and urbanization. The second half of the chapter deals with the meaning of poverty and urban poverty, which includes the historical perspectives of urban poverty. This is followed by a discussion on the theoretical background of urban poverty where different theories, including social transformation theory, the functionalist theory, and the conflict theory, will be discussed. Finally, urban poverty debates in different parts of the world are summarized.

Chapter 3: Urbanization and Urban Poverty in Bangladesh

Urbanization and urban poverty are closely linked as the former creates the latter. The hasty urbanization in Bangladesh over the last 20 years has accelerated the growth of urban poverty in major cities. Therefore, this chapter presents a discussion on the intensity and extent of urbanization in Bangladesh from a historical perspective. While analyzing the situation of urbanization, different issues, including the urban situation, urban growth, the proportion of urban population and share of GDP, have been given special prominence. Moreover, the issue of urban poverty has been discussed, highlighting the growth and impact of urban poverty on the economy of the country.

Chapter 4: Formation of Slums and Slum Upgradation Initiatives in Bangladesh

In the year 2008, the total urban population outstripped the rural population throughout the world. This majority of people who began to live in urban areas created an enormous amount of pressure on the cities, leading to a large number of slum population in most countries of the world. Like other countries, Bangladesh has also experienced the growth of slum population. Most importantly, people who are coming to the cities for their livelihoods do not have tenure of land, and thus, they begin to reside anywhere they find vacant. Thus, this chapter first explores why slums form globally and later in the context of Bangladesh. In addition, slum-upgrading initiatives in the country have been discussed briefly.

Chapter 5: Global Best Practices of Urban Slum Development Initiatives

Throughout the world, many governments and organizations have been working on the improvement of urban slums. All initiatives cannot be considered as best initiatives. To be the best, a project must be effective over a long period of time. The main argument is that best practice should have the applicability in organizations lacking successful reform. That is why academicians and development practitioners have stressed the importance of different indicators, including shared vision, a clear perception of the current reality, creativity and innovation, and learning through practicing modality, while featuring a best practice. Thus, this chapter discusses a number of best practices of slum development initiatives globally that have proved to be successful in their endeavor to ensure development for the slums in different countries of the world. In addition to highlighting different components of these programs, the chapter also discusses lessons that have been learnt for possible replication in other countries of the world.

Chapter 6: Urban Slum-Upgrading Best Practices in Bangladesh

People usually migrate from rural to urban areas (towns and cities) being compelled by factors like the growing number of landless households and lack of job opportunities. These people, who are already destitute, do not have a decent place to live. Finding no other alternative, they begin to live in the slums where they do not get access to different services, including water supply, sanitation, waste collection or infrastructure, which are being provided by municipalities. Thus, they fall prey to different kinds of disease, crime and natural disasters. In Bangladesh, different organizations, including the government, nongovernmental organizations, and donors have been implementing various initiatives for upgrading the living conditions of the people in slums and reducing poverty there. This chapter discusses several urban slum-upgrading best practices in Bangladesh and their impact on slum dwellers. In addition to this, the major challenges of slum upgrading have been discussed and possible ways forward have been suggested.

Chapter 7: Conclusion

Based on discussions in the earlier chapters, the conclusion is that "hasty" urbanization has augmented the growth of urban poverty in Bangladesh. The majority of the poor does not have affordable quality housing, and lives in slums. Different initiatives have been taken by different organizations in Bangladesh to upgrade slums in Bangladesh. Among them, many programs have been found to be very successful as they have brought a revolution in the slums of the country. The chapter concludes by setting out why these programs have become successful.

Conclusion

One of the major challenges that Bangladesh confronts in the twenty-first century is its hasty urbanization. Beginning in the 1990s, the process accelerated out of control and without the necessary planning or resources to make it work. For instance, the country's capital Dhaka has been named as one of the fastest-growing megacities in the world. The hasty urbanization has not only accelerated the urban population but also increased the total number of people living in poverty. The majority of the people that are poor live in slums with no land tenure or security, despite having the Constitutional guarantee of housing for all. These people do not get access to the basic services needed for a decent standard of living. Considering the miseries of the slum population, the Government of Bangladesh, like those of other developing countries, and international and national organizations, has been implementing slum development initiatives. This book explains the dynamics of urbanization, urban poverty and slum development and how we can use them to achieve better lives for the urban poor. Chapter 2 offers a discussion on the theoretical debates on urbanization and urban poverty.

References

Degaga, D. T. (2010). Some realities of the urban poor and their food security situations: A case study of Berta Gibi and Gemechu Safar in the city of Addis Ababa, Ethiopia. *Environment and Urbanization, 22*(1), 179–198.

Durand-Lasserve, A., & Royston, L. (2002). *Holding their ground: Secure land tenure for the urban poor in developing countries.* London: Earthscan.

https://www.ucl.ac.uk/dpu-projects/drivers_urb_change/urb_infrastructure/pdf_land%20tenure/WaterAid_Land_Tenure.pdf.

Islam, N. (2012, June 16–18). *Urbanization and urban governance in Bangladesh.* A background paper for the 13th annual global development conference on "urbanization & development: Delving deeper into the nexus", Budapest.
Islam, N. (2004). The poor's access to land and housing in Dhaka. Paper written for the World Bank, Dhaka Urban Poverty Study. Retrieved from https://www.researchgate.net/profile/Sohail_Ahmad2/publication/273608559_Housing_demand_and_housing_policy_in_urban_Bangladesh/links/56d3098608ae4d8d64a76d89/Housing-demand-and-housing-policy-in-urban-Bangladesh.pdf (accessed on 30/12/2019).
Jayarantne, K. A. (2009). *Draft strategy for improvement of tenure security of poor in UPPR towns in Bangladesh.* Dhaka: UNDP.
Jones, G. A. (Ed.). (2003). *Urban and markets in transition.* CD ROM. Cambridge, MA: Lincoln Institute of Land Policy.
Khan, S. P. (2007). *An exploratory study of slum development projects in Dhaka city: A case study of UBSDP and WATSAN.* An Unpublished Master Dissertation. BRAC University, Dhaka.
McGranahan, G., & Martine, G. (Eds.). (2014). *Urban growth in emerging economies: Lessons from the BRICS.* Abingdon: Routledge.
Mooya, M. M., & Chris, E. C. (2007). Informal urban property markets and poverty alleviation: A conceptual framework, *Urban Studies, 44*(1): 147–165.
Moser, C. (Ed.). (2007). *Reducing global poverty: The case for asset accumulation.* Washington, DC: Brookings Institution Press.
Mostafa, A. (n.d.). *Evolution of participatory and support based approach for strengthening tenure security, housing and community resilience.* A documentation of pilot project experience on secure tenure under partnership for poverty reduction (UPPR) project, UN-HABITAT, Bangladesh.
Panday, P. K. (2017). *Reforming urban governance in Bangladesh: The city corporation. The UK.* Cham: Palgrave Macmillan.
Saleh, A., & Khan, M. (2017). *Bangladesh urban housing dilemma.* Retrieved June 5, 2019, from http://blog.brac.net/reimagining-slums-innovative-solutions-to-bangladeshs-urban-housing-dilemma/.
Satterthwaite, D. (2003). The millennium development goals and urban poverty reduction: Grate expectations and nonsense statistics. *Environment and Urbanization, 15*(2), 179–190.
Shafi, S., & Payne, G. (2007). *Final report—Land tenure security and land administration in Bangladesh.* Dhaka: LPUPAP.
Tacoli, C. (2017). *Migration and inclusive urbanization.* Working Paper No. UN/POP/EGM/2017/6. United Nations expert group meeting on sustainable cities, human mobility and international migration. New York: Department of Economic and Social Affairs, United Nations Secretariat.
Tacoli, C., Bukhari, B., & Fischer, S. E. (2013). *Urban poverty, food security and climate change.* Human Settlements Working Papers, IIED, London.

The Constitution of Bangladesh (Modified up to 2016). Dhaka: Government of People's Republic of Bangladesh.

UNDP. (2006). *UPPR project technical annex*. Dhaka.

UN-HABITAT. (2003a). *The challenge of slums: Global report on human settlements 2003*. London: Earthscan.

UN-HABITAT. (2003b). *Guide to monitoring target 11: Improving the lives of 100 million slum dwellers: Progress towards the millennium development goals*. Nairobi: UN-HABITAT.

United Nations Human Settlements Program (UN-Habitat). (2013). *Sustainable cities and human settlements in the post-2015 UN development agenda*. Retrieved December 23, 2017, from http://sustainabledevelopment.un.org/content/documents/1653SustainableCities.pdf.

World Bank. (2006). *The Mumbai slum sanitation program: Partnering with slum communities for sustainable sanitation in a megalopolis*. Report No. 38456. Washington, DC: World Bank.

CHAPTER 2

Theoretical Debates on Urban Poverty

Introduction

Jones (2003) used three "transitions" to carry out research on the urban setting of different developing countries. According to him, these three transitions could be used as the foundation of contemporary research and policy design on urbanization. The first transition denotes the growing trend of urbanization of different developing countries. Considering the trends of the recent growth rate in urban population, Mooya and Chris (2007) estimated that cities would encompass almost 80% of the total urban population of the world by 2025. This astounding number in turn indicates the challenges that the world would face in the coming days due to this explosion in urban human populace (Durand-Lasserve and Royston 2002).[1]

Urbanization of poverty is the second transition propounded by Jones. In some countries, due to this growing trend of urbanization, the rate of urbanized poor would increase exponentially too; in fact, more than the rural areas, according to some estimates. For instance, the Department for International Development (2001) projected that the ratio of the urban populace living in different parts of Latin America, East and Central Europe, and Central Asia, would be two-thirds of the world, while the ratio would be a third to almost half in Africa. Asia supposedly would live

[1] For more details about the growing trend of urbanization, please go through Jones (2003), and Durand-Lasserve and Royston (2002).

P. K. Panday, *The Face of Urbanization and Urban Poverty in Bangladesh*, https://doi.org/10.1007/978-981-15-3332-7_2

in cities or towns by 2025. In his third transition, Jones (2003) puts greater emphasis on the rights of property in the development agenda. This sort of thinking is a reflection of the dominance of thinking of new institutional economics. Among different scholars and organizations, De Soto (2000), the World Bank (2001) and UNCHS-Habitat (2003) have been advocating for introducing property rights in developing countries. As an immediate consequence, several countries in recent times have begun providing land tenure security (Durand-Lasserve et al. 2007).

Herein, it may be noted that all the three transitions are interrelated. For instance, the growing trend of urbanization and poverty are directly related, while property rights do have a close relationship with the first two transitions. Thus, it is imperative to comprehend the issues of "Urbanization", "Poverty" and "Urban Poverty" from a deeper perspective.

Urbanization

In the last two decades, the "urbanization" has been of paramount importance as a developmental issue both in academics and among development practitioners. Thus, both scholars and development practitioners have looked to define the same from different perspectives. Before going into its details, it is important to understand a few key terms, including "Urban", "Urbanism" and "Urbanize".

When it comes to "urban", academicians have mostly tended to use the term to describe economic variables (i.e. the prevalence of nonagricultural occupation) or demographic characteristics (i.e. size and/or density) (Gibbs 1961). On the other hand, scholars like Jefferson (1909) and Wilcox (1926) used the term to indicate the density of the population. From the position of economic variables, scholars used the term to identify areas where an occupation of more than three-fourths of the entire population remain engaged in the nonagricultural sector, which is significantly developed, and where the difference between buildings is very small. Commonly, the term is used in contrast to rural, characterized by relatively low population, with an agriculture-based society. However, many scholars have opined that defining urban using a single criterion is not enough. Thus, they have used numerous criteria to define the term. For instance, Sorokin and Zimmerman (1929) using different criteria have come up with a "multiple" or "compound" definition of the term. They have distinguished urban from rural on grounds of occupation, size, density, heterogeneity, mobility, social differentiation, stratification, and the process of interaction of the populace at large.

On the other hand, Gibbs (1961: 14) stated "there is some hazard, on the theoretical level, in using a compound definition which mixes different universes of discourse." But at the same time, identification of an urban place using all criteria is a difficult task, as the accommodation of all criteria in one definition is next to impossible. However, there cannot be any universal definition of the term that possibly could be used in all countries. Nevertheless, the central point of all the definitions is that "urban" is considered as "settled areas" where more people live, and the density of the populace is high compared to rural areas. Additionally, it is appropriate for locating administrative facilities and functions. Most countries and people tend to use this broader and generic use of this term, whereby it is the administrative criterion, which serves as the very foundation of the definition. However, there are some who choose to use the population relation criterion (Buettner 2014; UN 2012).

The term "Urbanism", on the other hand, is used to denote the lifestyle that has close linkage with the activity, which in essence identifies with the spirit of city residence (Queen and Carpenter 1953). But, this is a narrow description of urbanism, as we cannot exclude the rural areas. Bergel (1955: 10) floated a view of the term as "a condition or set of circumstance". Fischer (1982: 23), on the other hand, defined urbanism as "the number of people living in and near a community". By this definition, he tried to identify the proximity of population concentration with each other, in addition to the size of the populace. He asserted that "people surrounding a community contribute to its urbanism along with the people living within it" (p. 23). In urban sociology, the term has been used to indicate the idiosyncratic social and cultural forms that grow in cities. Thus, defining urbanism is an easy task, as there are inherent multifaceted complexities within this term. Wirth (1938) chose to define this term by identifying some distinguishing features in the form of heterogeneity, a high amount of reliance of metropolitans upon others, the segmental feature of urban social relations, along with an erudition and shrewdness of the urban people. Of course, one may argue that the presence of these features can be found even among farmers, but predominantly these are seen in urban areas with variations in different country contexts. Finally, the term "urbanize" refers to the process of conversion from nonurban into urban. The US Bureau of Census (2002: 1) defined an "urbanized" area as "a place and the adjacent densely settled surrounding territory that together comprise a minimum population of 50,000 people", where the "densely settled surrounding territory" is defined as "one or more contiguous block having a population density of at least 1000 people per square mile".

The above-mentioned three interrelated and very important terms lead us to commence our discussion on urbanization by saying that the term refers to the movement of people from rural to urban areas. Thompson (1935: 189) stated that "urbanization is characterized by movements of people from small communities concerned chiefly or solely with agriculture to other communities generally larger, whose activities are predominantly centered in government, trade, manufacture, or allied interests". On the other hand, while featuring urbanization, Hauser and Duncan (1959) stressed the importance of the changing pattern of distribution of population that would involve an upsurge in the absolute size of the urban population. They also paid attention to the development of urban settlements or places with a focus on the swelling concentration of the population in such places. Thompson's definition of the term has been criticized, as he stressed the importance of the movement as an inevitable condition of urbanization. But, there are instances where urbanization has been conceived without movement in different parts of the world, as natural increase of population in urban places and changes in occupation in rural areas have fostered the growth of urbanization. Despite the differences in the definition of the term, it can be stated that urbanization is a process that denotes changes in the size, density and heterogeneity of cities over time. The process of urbanization, by and large, may be linked to the process of industrialization and the movement of both population and resources from the rural to the urban areas. However, it is important to mention that the process of urbanization in developing countries does not depend on industrialization (Davis 2006).

But, there is hardly any scope to use urbanization and urban population growth synonymously, as the two are different despite the fact that they are often conflated. The value of urban and rural population at the same rate will not be considered as urbanization, since there has to be a rising urban share of the population if it has to be "urbanized". On the other hand, an increasing urban share without an upsurge in the urban population can actually lead to urban population growth due to urbanization, where the rate of urban population growth equals the proportion of urbanization. Since population is on the rise in most urbanized countries, making a differentiation between the shares of urban population influenced by urbanization and the portion that is caused due to the growth of population is not a difficult task. Roughly, the ratio of urbanization and overall population is found to be equal to the ratio of growth of the urban population in itself (Tacoli et al. 2014). This substantiates that urbanization and urban population growth are strongly correlated. Based on the discussion of different definitions of urbanization, we argue that urbanization is the process through which the emergence and growth of cities are expedited. Importantly, this isn't dependent on the definition of urban, but does have a strong relationship with the dynamics of agglomeration of an individual. The term also denotes the growth of the share of the populace that lives in urban areas, as opposed to rural areas.

Causes of Growth of Urbanization

The world's urbanization rate increased to about 50% in 2012, while the ration distribution increased by just about 30% from 1950 (United Nations 2012). Countries like China and Korea have attained a high-income growth along with an increasing trend of urbanization, as historically the rate of urbanization in these countries has been very high. On the other hand, countries like Pakistan, Bangladesh, Haiti and the Democratic Republic of the Congo have experienced a steady growth rate of urbanization despite the existence of massive poverty and unstable political situation (Glaeser 2013).

Developing countries have possibly witnessed the biggest spurt in terms of the pace of urbanization. This growth rate resembles the process of urbanization in various industrialized nations. Moreover, as compared to earlier times, the process of urbanization in recent times, especially for developing countries, seems to have a close relation with the increasing rate of per capita income. One cannot obviously say that urbanization has a strong correlation with per capita income (Acemoglu et al. 2002); however, scholars like Henderson (2010), Glaeser (2013), and Jedwab and Vollrath (2015) have indeed acknowledged that economic development and urbanization are effectively interrelated, albeit in a vicious circle. Michaels et al. (2012) have also concurred with this proposition. Further, they stated that through the developmental process of a country, its people do tend to travel toward cities from rural areas, whereby they look to migrate their agricultural activities into urban areas, while also getting engaged in manufacturing and service activities. These transformed urban sectors tend to experience a high rate of output, and the effect of accumulation is thought to be accelerated economic growth in the future (Duranton 2008; Glaeser and Gottlieb 2009). Thus, one may safely assume that no country can grow economically without the process of urbanization (Tacoli 2017).

Additionally, one may also add that the intensity and the state of economic, social and political changes do strongly influence the process of urbanization, obviously in varying ways and degrees. The degree of urbanization has led scholars to examine the factors that affect the process of urbanization (McGranahan and Satterthwaite 2014). The growing rate of improved opportunity induced rural–urban migration, higher opportunities for jobs in cities, or shrinking job markets in rural areas have intensified the growth of urbanization, especially in low- and middle-income countries. In the last 60 years, people's movement toward cities vis-à-vis its impact on the dispersal of economic opportunities has accelerated economic growth in different parts of the world. Today, the service sectors along with the industry at large comprise 97% of the world's GDP. The rate of active population working in these sectors is around 65%. Most importantly, these activities are all based on urban areas (Satterthwaite et al. 2010; Tacoli 2017). At the same time, it may be noted that urbanization as a consequence of people's movement toward cities cannot be the only cause, if one were to indicate long-term movement of the rural dwellers in urban areas permanently, due to a few reasons. First, it is important to note that complex migratory movements between both rural and urban centers initiate the process of urbanization. Second, the rural–urban migration is what calls for extensions of urban boundaries, which go on to create new cities. Third, higher rates of natural population growth in urban areas do also influence the process of urbanization (Tacoli et al. 2014).

Along with industrialization, the process of urbanization is often intensified by the growth of large cities. Sub-Saharan Africa and Asia are two continents where the growth of large urban cities is very high. In these places, the demographic and socioeconomic importance of small urban cities has remained underrated due to differences in definitions and administrative status. However, these growing cities could play a pivotal role in regional advancement by supporting rural transformation through diversification of rural household income and reinforcement of the food system (Tacoli and Agergaard 2017). Herein, we should not forget that these small cities play the dominant role in developing curiosity in regional methods to territorial expansion (UCLG 2016). However, rapid growth of urbanization in most of the developing countries has also proportionately accelerated the growth of unplanned, underserved neighborhoods with a high concentration of poor people (McGranahan and Martine 2014). Consequently, urban poverty has become an inseparable part of the overall process of urbanization. The following section sheds light on the meaning of poverty vis-à-vis urban poverty.

Meaning of Poverty

Defining poverty using a universal approach is an arduous task due to its inherent complexities. It reminds us of the old story of three blind persons' first-time experience of coming across an elephant. The elephant was perceived as a wall when the first man touched the animal, while the second person identified it as a tree by touching the leg of the animal. The third person having touched the large springy trunk termed the animal as a large mole. In other words, this story explains the larger truth that an individual does have the tendency to describe something based on his/her understanding, experiences and predilection. This story has been used here to show that reaching an agreement on the definition of poverty is tough. As a matter of fact, to arrive at an agreement on the meaning of poverty does require us to read through different contested definitions of the term along with its multiple, complicated perspectives. Briefly, the term (i.e. poverty) may be understood as an individual, societal, countrywide or regional problem.

According to Friedman (1996), poverty is the process through which the poor become socially, economically, politically and psychologically disempowered due to the lack of access to sufficient resources required to maintain their livelihood. The absence of a clear political agenda, along with the lack of scope for the poor to raise their voices in the political process, has been arbitrated as psychological disempowerment. In fact, psychological disempowerment has been labelled as poor people's presumed sagacity of tidbit and flabby compliance to authority (Friedman 1996). On the other hand, Oppenheim and Harker (1996) have denoted poverty as a person's substantial, social and emotive miseries. Most importantly, a person's inability to spend on daily necessities of life, including food, heating and clothing as compared to his/her average income can be termed as an impoverished condition. The sagacity of anxiety limits the ability of the people to live as they wish. In this situation, they are forced to lead a miserable life with many adverse effects, including illness, lack of education, insecure homes and a lack of retirement benefits. Sen (1981) stressed on stubborn hunger when there are copious food stocks while defining poverty. Thus, the application of different mechanisms by different groups has been encouraged to gain access to and control over food. He further added that peoples' access to food is not guaranteed even when there is adequate food. In order to ensure accessibility of food to those who are in dire need, the role of institutional interaction cannot be ignored, as institutions could deprive them of exercising rights to freedom, choice and actions (Sen 1984, 1999).

Poverty has also been explained through several important dimensions. For instance, Narayan et al. (2000) in their classic book entitled 'Voices of the Poor' state at first that poverty should not be thought of as the lack of only one single thing. Instead, it should be considered in relation to hunger, which in turn has a close relationship with the availability of food. Second, while defining poverty, they state that different psychological dimensions like powerlessness, voicelessness, dependency, shame and humiliation need to be considered. Third, they state that poverty does have a strong relationship with people's lack of access to basic infrastructural facilities including roads (in rural areas), transportation and clean water. Fourth, for the poor, schooling does not seem to be sufficiently significant, despite a widespread thirst for literacy that arises as they realize the importance of education, which they believe would drive them out of poverty. Fifth, the prevalence of poor health and illness at places where the poor live in turn tend to aggravate poverty. Furthermore, it relates to the costs of health care and income loss due to illness. Although the poor express their concern about income but remains focused on the management of properties in the form of physical, human, social and environmental. In many areas, this vulnerability has a gender dimension.[2]

According to Townsend (1979: 31) "Individuals, families and groups in the population can be said to be in poverty when they lack the resources to obtain the types of diet, participate in the activities and have the living conditions and amenities which are customary …. in the societies to which they belong."

Providing emphasis on absolute and relative poverty, Santarelli and Figini (2002: 4) have computed poverty based on an individual whose income remains under a conventional threshold of the poverty line. On the other hand, Atoloye (cited in Gold 2006: 283) defined poverty

[2] For more detail about several dimensions of poverty see Narayan et al. (2000).

through the level of deficiency, which comprises of some deficits and insufficiencies in some fundamental needs of humankind, which tend to thwart people to attain a globally acceptable level of security.

Excluding the overall society, absolute poverty measures refer entirely to the happiness of the poor. Anyanwu (1997: 101) stated "relative poverty relates to the situation of an individual or household compared to the average income in the country". In other words, the absolute real income is used to measure the state of poverty. Santarelli and Figini (2002: 6) came up with comprehensive methodologies to calculate poverty, where they used a few indicators like (1) the headcount poverty indices (HPI), given by the percentage of the total population of individuals (household) with the number of income units (consumption) falling below the poverty line; (2) the gap poverty index (GPI), which calculates the average level of intake of the poor with respect to the poverty line; (3) and the family of indices (FGI), which concurrently ponders the percentage of the poor, their average intake, vis-à-vis the distribution of the intake among the poor. The discussion above leads us to understand poverty as opposed to prosperity and development. Thus, poverty is a situation where people do not have adequate capacity to maintain their livelihood in a standard way. However, there are differences of opinion among scholars in terms of benchmarking the minimum standard of living.

Meaning of Urban Poverty

For more than a century, urban poverty has remained an issue of discussion of sociologists and political scientists. The ever-increasing theoretical attention to urban poverty has invited discussion on the causes, consequences and solutions to this problem. The term had been carrying its greatest influence on the people of Africa since the 1960s. For instance, if we look at the growth of the extremely poor in Africa, it is apparent that these regions experienced a growth rate of 164% during 1970–1980 (Wilson 1987). This increase facilitated the growth of unemployment, dependency on government support, high birth rate, along with corruption and crime.

In the midst of uncertainty and complexity regarding the definition of urban poverty, two broad approaches seem to be the most common among scholars. One refers to a conventional economic approach, where the poor are identified through social indicators like income/consumption, etc. (Wratten 1995; Satterthwaite 1995). The other, primarily propounded by anthropologists and social planners, refers to poor people using the perception of nonmaterial dispossession and social discrepancy (Islam et al. 1997).

Conventional Economic Approach

Poverty in the conventional economic approach refers to the incapacity of attaining a basic income required to maintain a minimal standard of living, measured through indicators like food, housing, education, medical treatment, health, security and sanitation (Pigou 1952). Poverty in this sense may be articulated as the incapability of a person to bear these expenses (i.e. food, housing, education, etc.). Herein, it is the income level of an individual, which is prominent, based on which he or she would be able to cater to other necessary facilities and services. Jackson (1972) concurred with this focus on the income level of an individual. He defined poverty as a lack of income, which is required to maintain the cost of bearing expenses of meeting basic needs, which in turn creates a sense of deprivation among people in society. He added that there is indeed a relationship between the flow of services vis-à-vis the flow of food consumption. The flow of services originates from some parameters like housing, clothes, education, etc., which are absolutely necessary for social life. Thus, this is a conventional viewpoint of poverty that stresses on the importance of earning, which helps people meet their basic needs.

However, this conventional dimension of poverty does not put sufficient emphasis on the nutrition value of food requirement; rather, it describes a situation in poverty (Islam et al. 1997). This lacuna has raised the issue of determining the "minimum standard of living".

Taking into consideration the shortcoming in the conventional definition of poverty, Ojha (1970), Dandekar and Rath (1971), and Ahluwalia (1978) endeavored to construe poverty in terms of food nutrients and calorie intake. However, there is a risk involved in the process of defining poverty in terms of shortage of food nutrients, since it may be synonymously treated with malnourishment (Islam et al. 1997).

Absolute and Relative Poverty

Poverty can be explained through absolute and relative viewpoints. When we talk about absolute poverty, it denotes a person's incapability to meet the minimum requirements of life. Conversely, an individual having an income below a certain amount, which is believed to be inadequate for meeting his or her minimum requirement of life, is recognized as being poor. Definition of poverty in absolute terms states that needs are presumed to be static, just at a level, which may be considered "adequate" in order to provide subsistence, basic household equipment and expenditure on essential services (i.e. water, shelter, health, education and transport) (Wratten 1995). However, the advancement of technology in the form of improved ways of life could get adjusted to the definition of poverty from time to time.

Relative poverty, on the other hand, signifies income inequality in society. Townsend (1979) was the first to develop the concept of relative poverty as an alternative approach to measure poverty in itself, criticizing some of the absolute levels of minimum needs. All the members of a society may not have equal income, assets and facilities of community life. In this view, it is reflected that poverty inflicts removal or barring from active membership of society where people are found to be comparatively deprived from access to different amenities of life (Wratten 1995). Townsend (1979: 36) further pointed out "… the conditions of life—that is the diets, amenities, standards and services—which allow them to play the roles, participate in the relationships and follow the customer behavior, which is expected of them by virtue of their membership of society". One of the important aspects of relative poverty is the presumption that people's needs are influenced by the society in which they live and belong to. Thus, it is very difficult to claim that the needs of the people would indeed remain absolute under all contexts.

Definitions Based on Social Indicators

Since there seems to be a tendency among scholars to avoid highlighting the problem associated with rural–urban price differentiation, the social indicators are usually used to identify the differences between the welfare of both the rural and the urban populace. The application of these indicators may come up with some conflicting stories about the pattern of deprivation, which was happened in the case of absolute poverty. Due to the inaccuracy of these indicators when making a differentiation between the deprivation levels, scholars have primarily tended to rely on the income and consumption measures as the key variables to define poverty—this despite the fact that this single indicator suffers from drawbacks while defining well-being of people (Wratten 1995).

Composite poverty indices that include a number of slanted combined variables have been developed to define poverty by overcoming the deficits of a single indicator. For example, UNDP used income, literacy and life expectancy as measurement criteria of poverty in its Human Development report. While calculating poverty, different variables have been accumulated into a single measurement criterion on a scale of zero to one. Using this score, UNDP ranked different countries based on their poverty condition. Herein, it may be noted that UNDP's index is not the only benchmark by which countries are ranked based on their poverty condition. There are other indices, including the Physical Quality of Life Index,[3] the Food Security Index and the Relative Welfare Index, through which the poverty situation of a country is defined, and based on which, they are ranked.[4] Unfortunately, it is difficult to claim that a particular index is perfect, because each of the indices does tend to use a limited number of variables, while calculating the poverty line.

Historical Perspective of Urban Poverty

The debate on urban poverty first began in the Southern—followed by the—Northern, part of the world. If we look at the development literature of an ancient period, it would be evident that there were discriminations between the rural poor vis-à-vis the urban population, which has been assumed to be better off. Thus, the relations between urbanization, the extension of capitalism and poverty have remained as the central point of development literature. On the other hand, different challenges like inner-city or peripheral urban social housing estates or regional and sectoral redundancy and income disparity have remained as the core of poverty analysis in the North. In this region, low attention was paid to the investigation of the urban–rural division (Wratten 1995).

During the colonial period, all problems that were assumed to be relating to the South were expected to be resolved through the growth of urbanization and labor transformation toward high output from low output within the modern industrial arenas (Lewis 1958). However, such expectations of this two-sector growth model came under serious questioning during the 1970s. As the decades passed, the benefits of

[3] To know more about the Physical Quality of Life Index, see Morris (1979).

[4] For details about the Food Security Index and the Relative Welfare Index, see Idriss et al. (1992).

modernization policies did not reach those rural places, where the larger populace actually lived. Lipton (1977), through his great piece of work "Urban Bias", criticized his government's taxation and expenditure policies that were considered city-friendly. He insisted that rural areas were being deprived of various opportunities available to urban areas. He attributed this to be among the main reasons for not being able to alleviate poverty. Considering the importance of the "urban bias" in Lipton's thesis, development agencies accepted it as one of the mainstream views in the 1970s and 1980s. Being influenced by this thesis, development theorists reoriented poverty alleviation strategies to improve the livelihood status and living conditions of the people living in rural areas, primarily across "Third World Countries". From the mid-1980s onward, these efforts were reinforced through structural adjustment policies, whereby efforts were made to remove supports that were previously provided to urban consumers and thus there was hike in prices of market values that favored rural producers (Wratten 1995).

Through different types of researches that were conducted in the 1980s and 1990s, different types came out in the degree and intensity of poverty within the urban sector in the Third World. However, the research findings were criticized on the ground that the poverty situation was inferior in deprived city slums as compared to rural communities (Amis and Lloyd 1990). Consequently, urban poverty as a developmental issue attained immense prominence among academicians and development practitioners, leading them to work toward urban growth. Recognizing the importance of the issue, the World Bank in its policy paper mentioned that "... by the late 1980s, urban per capita incomes in some countries had reverted to 1970 levels and in some countries to 1960 levels" (World Bank 1991: 32).

The Eugene Comprehensive Lands Assessment (ECLA) estimated the state of poverty in both urban and rural areas of ten Latin American countries, which were heavily influenced by the urban bias thesis of the 1980s. Surprisingly, the ratio of poor urban households in Latin America increased significantly from 1981 to 1986. As regards the number of people under absolute poverty, the poverty situation in urban areas turned out to be one of the great challenges for seven Latin Americans countries. It may be noted herein that during that period, a significant increase was observed in the number of urban poor, rising to about 58% (in 1986) as opposed to 48% (in 1980) (Feres and Leon 1990).

In the early 1970s, Latin American (LATAM) countries also experienced a steady decline in urban wages This decrease was due to a decline of real income levels along with a general exacerbation in urban employment safety and welfare, including employer housing. Countries like Tanzania, Uganda and Ghana, for instance, experienced a sharp reduction in the urban–rural income differential (Amis and Lloyd 1990). The wave that began in Latin American countries also flowed through Bangladesh, which also witnessed a deterioration in urban living standards and a tapering gap between poverty in rural and urban areas (Francis 1991).

Since the early twentieth century, most people in industrial Europe and North America began to live in towns and cities. This tendency influenced scholars to re-conduct comprehensive research on poverty.[5] Nonetheless, researchers from the Northern countries were not convinced to identify "urban poverty" as separate from "poverty", as they were of the opinion that the process of determination of poverty had already been influenced by the urban images of poverty. Nonetheless, despite the limited enthusiasm of Northern researchers, the issue of 'urban poverty' received enough attention among researchers in the UK and the USA as an important dimension to discuss deficit in inner-city areas or peripheral social housing estates. However, a different picture was observed in Europe, where urban or inner-city poverty was viewed as an element of the all-embracing issue of marginalization.

Theoretical Background

There are many ways of looking at a particular phenomenon, issue or event. The method of describing a phenomenon from diverse perspectives is called an approach or a perspective. Like other aspects of our social life, poverty can be described from the perspectives of four approaches: Social Transformation Theory, Functionalist Theory, Conflict Theory, and Structural Perspective/Institutional Discrimination. These four approaches have been briefly discussed in the following section.

Social Transformation Theory

According to Offiong (2001: 124), poverty is "functional and persists because it performs certain functions to certain groups of people". We

[5] To know more about traditional research on urban poverty, see Seebohm (1901).

observed the existence of poverty in the economy seeing a large number of low-wage workers taking perilous, indecorous and unwanted jobs that are not undertaken by the rich. Poverty, along with the movement of financial capital, pledges organizations that they will be placed in an advantageous position to further reduce labor costs. True, government intervention could forcefully bring changes in the working conditions of the labor force in developing countries. Herein, the governments could look to improve the environmental situation, while enacting laws that secure workers' rights and protection. In turn, this would ensure that wages are kept at a minimum level, while workers' rights are also preserved (Offiong 2001).

Poverty not only facilitates the formation of a low-wage workforce, but it also contributes to the construction of a prepared market for low-quality products forsaken by rich nations. Due to the persistence of poverty, we witness the mobilization of human capital, seeking of employment by high-skilled workers in richer nations, which causes unwarranted brain drain for the developing world. Offiong (2001) also exemplified how poverty supports the making of trades that could earn profit from the welfare system.

Beyond the national level, poverty compels the government of poor countries to work according to the will of the rich countries at an international level. The rich countries always dictate the economy and politics of the poor in the name of transfer of goods or capital (Offiong 2001).[6] Thus, it may be stated that poverty can transform the social and political settings of poverty-ridden countries.

The Functionalist Theory

Sociologists and social scientists still recognize functionalism as the oldest, but dominant, theory that could illustrate poverty well. Two significant ideologies within this theory include the use of scientific methods to the impartial social world, and the application of ontology to differentiate between individual organizations and society. This approach also puts emphasis on macro-level issues that affect income disparity. Most importantly, the theorists favoring the functionalist approach remain more concerned about employment opportunities and the wage gap between individuals (Guest et al. 2006). A functionalist approach has both positive

[6] For more details on Social Transformation Theory, please see Offiong (2001).

and negative viewpoints in terms of poverty. Interestingly, both views consider family structure as an important factor causing poverty. Of course, there are opposite views as well. For instance, Murray (1984) considered that poor people could still survive without working if there was a welfare system in the country. That is why it is often said that a culture of poverty is reinforced by the support that it gets within a welfare system (Murray 1984). Most importantly, wage gap between individuals creates poverty, and is caused by varying employment opportunities within a country.

The Conflict Theory

The main thrust of the social conflict theory has been derived from the ideas of Karl Marx (1818–1853). Marx's main focus was on a materialist elucidation of history, a dialectical method of analysis with a critical stance on existing social arrangements, and political programs of revolution or, at least, reform. Denying the functionalists' point of view that condemns family structure as one of the prominent causes of poverty, conflict theorists considered poverty as a desire of the middle and upper classes in the society. Briefly, they believed that poverty exists only because these groups of people want it to exist. Further, these theorists were of the opinion that employers intentionally exploit the working poor in order to make a profit for their business and live a prosperous life. The sufferings of the unemployed remain the same as well-off employers, who do not want to carry new businesses that could possibly reduce unemployment, as they are reluctant to pay more taxes. The main thesis of the conflict approach on poverty is grounded on the postulation that social life is a constant skirmish where members of powerful groups intend to keep their control on scarce resources that include social, economic, and political superiority (cited in Kemp 1994).

Structural Perspective/Institutional Discrimination

Eitzen (2000: 200) stated that "the real explanation of why the poor are poor is that they made the mistake of being born to the wrong parents, in the wrong section of town, in the wrong industry, or in the wrong racial or ethnic group". The poor live in such a structural situation in society that itself is the main cause of poverty, more so due to institutional discrimination, entrenched in the usual ways of doing things, predominant outlooks and expectancy, and recognized structural preparations. Such a situation deprives the poor from different amenities of life including education, health and sanitation, that is, according to Eitzen, the institutional structure that pushes people toward poverty.

The discussions above suggest that scholars have tried to discuss poverty from different perspectives. Common among them is that they perceived poverty as the deprivation of a certain group of people from different rights (e.g. education, health care, sanitation). Moreover, most of them opined that the rich always want to keep these people under poverty. Interestingly, in some cases, family structure has also been identified as one of the prominent causes of poverty. Finally, the role of the institutional structure has been identified as another main cause of poverty.

Categorization of Poverty

Poverty can take different shapes globally. Types of poverty have been categorized based on the type of the political economy of a country, while the Gross National Production (GNP) per capita of a country has been considered as the base of the second category. The basis of the third category of poverty is the classification of a First World and Third World. All these categories of poverty have been briefly discussed below in terms of a First World–Third World classification.

Poverty Based on Political Economy

Considering the different types of political economy that exist in different parts of the world, Wilson (1996: 18) identified five categories of political economy where poverty exists as a dominant issue. The first refers to a situation where most of the people spend their lives living under the poverty line due to scarce internal resources. Classic examples of this type of political economy include China, India and Rwanda. The second category is where a particular pattern of growth is considered as the poverty that might help the reduction of the poverty situation as well. Malaysia, South Africa and Latin America may be considered as classic examples of this category. The third category states that poverty is triggered by an apparent letdown of the state. Eastern Europe, Nigeria along with a few other African countries are classic examples of this class. The fourth category alludes to a place where there is a reawakening of poverty, coupled with genuine endeavors to change the welfare state. Individuals living within these classifications remained underestimated in the mainstream of the political economy in their nations. Canada and numerous nations in Western Europe are instances of this type. The fifth and last classification is the place where there is a transformed attack on poor people. Hereby, the outcome is combined with dynamic strides to disassemble social measures, initially intended to shield natives from the most exceedingly terrible desolates of destitution. The USA, the UK and New Zealand are instances of this type (Wilson 1996).

Poverty in Terms of GNP Per Capita

There are a few nations that can be classified based on their GNP per capita. This standard, be that as it may, does not uncover anything about the conveyance of salary, and should, along these lines, be enhanced by the level of disparity as estimated by Gini-Coefficient (Todaro 1994).

Poverty in Terms of First- World–Third World Classification

Considering this characterization, Wratten (1995: 12) contended, "poverty in the North is less hazardous than in the South and is, as a rule, a minority issue. In the North, the Nordic way to deal with living conditions speaks to a unique commitment to the stock of knowledge on poverty". As indicated by this methodology, poverty must be noticeable, and should not consider feelings of individuals about poverty itself; instead, it should be considered from the perspective of their experience about their life. Thus the approach of poverty, consequently, comprises views of pay-related estimation and living conditions. Ringen (1988) contends that the perception of income is just an unforeseen proof to poverty. Extra analysis is associated with the actual incapacity to arrive at the minimum standard of living in the absence of adequate resources.

Wratten (1995: 12) claimed, "in the South, the majority still fails to attain a minimum satisfactory standard of living". It is due to the incapacity of society to ensure a supply of means that are required to attain a satisfactory standard of living. This is witnessed predominantly in Asia and Africa where malnourishment or a "dearth of food" approach to poverty is useful.

Urban Poverty Debate in Different Parts of the World

In many parts of the world, academicians have identified poverty as a political issue, as power and interest groups tend to influence the patterns of distribution. That is why, poverty analysis sometimes is considered as an issue, which is territorially challenged (Wilson 1996).

Discussions of poverty within the Third World stem from talks on both development and underdevelopment. The definition of development, therefore, carries special significance in this context. Considering the people-centric approach, the African National Congress (ANC) (1994) stated that development is related to people and not objects. This type of understanding does have significant inference when it comes to identifying strategies looking to reduce poverty.

It has been widely argued that any attempt to understand poverty and its possible solution must be based on a wider body of knowledge gathered from a general field of development. These understandings would go a long way in helping someone aspiring to understand a specific instance of poverty. Herein, we may add that the likelihood of dipping poverty through an actual restructuring policy, for instance, as a good example.

When the populist and technocratic model of development accelerates the tempo of development, the vicious circle of poverty is further engendered (Petmesidou and Tsoulouvis 1994). The main premise of the populist model is that growing public expenditure that accelerates social and political instability effectively reduces economic growth, and increases social conflict. On the other hand, the technological model affirms that in order to attain a high growth rate, one has to sacrifice social justice and political participation that eventually accelerate polarization and unrest (Petmesidou and Tsoulouvis 1994). Conversely, Wilson (1996) advocated in favor of the application of different theories in order to measure the state of poverty vis-à-vis the importance that is to be given to better understand poverty in different parts of the world.

For instance, the poverty situation in Europe has been described by two theoretical traditions. First, the Anglo-Saxon tradition has been used to describe the poverty situation, wherein the main concern is a distributional issue with special focus on the lack of scarcity of resources at the disposal of the household or individual. The second approach is the continental or intellectual tradition, grounded on the relationship pattern between scarce social participation, and the problem of integrating the poor into society at large. This concept of "poverty as social exclusion" has primarily been used in the Nordic countries, where the government uses the theory of marginalization and underclass in order to measure the state of poverty within the country (Wilson 1996).

Miller and Korenman (1994) identified a number of causes of poverty, while describing its state in the USA. These include demographic causes, neighborhood effects, cultural causes, and labor markets (e.g. human capital, mechanization, macro or Keynesian explanations, immigration ebbs and flows and welfare disincentives). On the other hand, poverty in South Asia has been described by Silva and Athukorala (1996: 65–66) using the following four theoretical frameworks:

(a) The neoclassical approach, with market-led development
(b) The political economy approach, focusing on the history, and the creation of poverty through conflict of interests
(c) The culture of poverty approach, which tends to blame the victim, and reinforce the status quo
(d) The participatory approach, whereby the energies of the poor themselves are harnessed to alleviate their plight

The discussion above suggests that there is no theoretical approach that could be considered as being the best through which poverty situations could be better described worldwide, since the context of each country is different. That is why different approaches have been used in different parts of the world. However, there are a few common features, which possibly could help in some sort of generalization, for instance, the theory on social power structure, or peoples' participation, availability of resources and/or other cultural perspectives.

Imminent Guidelines for Urban Poverty Reduction

Based on the discussions thus far, a few issues could be considered while looking for future direction in poverty alleviation. This is important because the shape and intensity of poverty has been changing all the time. Thus, in order to be prepared for dealing with issues of poverty, the following directions need to take taken into consideration:

1. An individual household's means of survival vis-à-vis its scope for adapting to diverse coping strategies must be considered with great

importance while making an attempt to analyze poverty. For instance, an analysis of household consumption, and the type of gender relation may possibly help us to carry forward any discussion in this regard. Additionally, it is important to bear in mind that we need to go beyond the consideration of income-based view of poverty. Instead, we need to understand susceptibility, prerogatives and social segregation, which encompass the importance of assets, along with the processes of exclusion.

2. Further, it is important to add that extant literature on urban development has stressed significantly on the role of governance, institutions and partnerships, be it with individuals, households, communities, voluntary and nongovernmental organizations, private enterprises, investors, along with government agencies in the process of alleviating poverty. Importantly, one must note that in order to foster partnerships, we need to identify gender-sensitive mechanisms, where both men and women would be involved to identify their needs and plans. Since the scale and magnitude of poverty are very complex, governments should pay more attention to strengthen both national and local capacity-building institutions, so that they impart effective and efficient training in local languages, given the gender-sensitiveness and the inclusion of all actors.
3. In order to ensure sustainable urban development, it is important to identify participatory forms of urban partnership that would create scope for both women and men to get involved at all stages of the development process. In terms of rights, it is again the prerogative of both women and men to have control on resources, so that they could contribute to the betterment of their individual well-being, as well as the well-being of their respective households, communities, and the country at large. Herein, it is imperative to reiterate that participation as empowerment refers to a process through which people get themselves organized, possibly in groups/clusters within cities. They identify and articulate their interests, bargain with the city officials to get their interests included in the city plans, and thereby look to bring changes in the life of the city dwellers (Beall 1996). There is also sufficient scope for conducting further research on the pivotal role that women could play in this endeavor. Further research could also be conducted on citizenship, democratization and decentralization and their interrelationship with regard to strengthening the framework of urban governance.

4. Another important aspect of poverty alleviation and urban development includes the point of sustainability of the city environment. This may be another focal area of future research, whereby one could look to explore the gender in relation to urban environment and poverty within the purview of urban development.
5. One of the salient issues that has become an important aspect of urban development and poverty reduction is social unrest and violence that starts at the household level and beyond (Moser 1995). More research could be conducted on this issue.
6. Each nation's constitution does provide people with the right to live a sustainable life, free from poverty. This has a strong relationship with three basic components of urban poverty. The first component includes the source of income; the second includes the rights of livelihood of migrants, child labor, landless, laborers, women, minorities, and the marginalized, who are obligated to face discernment, susceptibility and powerlessness; even in the age of globalization and structural reforms, they lack access to basic resources. The third component includes the protection and empowerment of the poor in the urban areas who seem to be the most vulnerable. These issues need to be understood well to face the challenges of urban poverty.

Conclusion

We have seen in this chapter that the rapid growth of urbanization has intensified the acceleration of urban poverty in different countries. Since urban economics are mainly cash-based, insufficient regular income has become one of the most important dimensions of urban poverty. Due to low income levels, many urban dwellers are forced to live in congested dwellings and/or temporary hovels, which are mostly illegal. These people lack the basic necessities. They also grieve from supplementary problems in the form of lack of policing, which often compels them to experience violence, volatility and insecurity. Further, they lack the financial independence, which often tends to deprive them even of exercising their voting rights. Briefly, these people are caught in a vicious circle of deprivation and poverty, which makes their life risky for even basic living. The next chapter sheds light on the history and interrelation between urbanization and urban poverty specifically in Bangladesh.

References

Acemoglu, D., Johnson, S., & Robinson, J. A. (2002). Reversal of fortune: Geography and institutions in the making of the modern world income distribution. *The Quarterly Journal of Economics, 117*(4), 1231–1294.

African National Congress (ANC). (1994). *The reconstruction and development program*. Johannesburg: Ravan Press.

Ahluwalia, A. (1978). An intra-cultural investigation of susceptibility to 'perspective' and 'non-perspective' spatial illusions. British Journal of Psychology. 69 (2): 233–241.

Amis, P. and Lloyd, P. (1990). *Housing Africa's urban poor*. Manchester and New York: Manchester University Press.

Anyanwu, J. C. (1997). *Poverty in Nigeria: Concepts and measurement and determinants*. Nigerian economic society selected paper for the annual conference on poverty alleviation in Nigeria (pp. 93–120).

Beall, J. (1996). Participation in the city: Where do women fit in? *Gender and Development, 4*(1), 9–16.

Bergel, E. E. (1955). *Urban sociology*. New York: Mc-Graw Hill.

Buettner, T. (2014). Urban estimates and projections at the United Nations: The strengths, weaknesses and underpinnings of the world urbanization prospects. *Spatial Demography, 3*(2), 91–108.

Dandekar, V. M., & Rath, N. (1971). *Poverty in India*. Poona: Indian School of Political Economy.

Davis, M. (2006). *Planet of slums*. New York: Verso.

Department for International Development. (2001). *Meeting the challenge of poverty in urban areas*. Strategies for achieving the international development target, the UK. Retrieved January 12, 2017, from https://www.ucl.ac.uk/dpu-projects/drivers_urb_change/official_docs/DFID_Strategy_Paper_urb_pov.pdf.

De Soto, H. (2000). The mystery of capital: Why capitalism triumphs in the west and fails everywhere else. New York, NY: Basic Books.

Durand-Lasserve, A., & Royston, L. (2002). Holding their ground: Secure land tenure for the urban poor in D]developing countries. London: Earthscan Publications.

Durand-Lasserve, A., Fernandes E., Payne, G., & Rakodi, G. (2007). Social and economic impacts of land titling programs in urban and peri-urban areas: A review of the literature. Retrieved February 13, 2018, from file:///C:/Users/Asus/Downloads/Social_and_economic_impacts_of_land_titling_progra.pdf.

Duranton, G. (2008). Cities: Engines of growth and prosperity for developing countries? Commission of Growth and Development. The International Bank for Reconstruction and Development. Washington DC: The World Bank.

Eitzen, D. (2000). *Social problems*. Boston: Allyn and Bacon.

Feres, J. C. and Leon, A. (1990). The magnitude of poverty in Latin America. CEPAL Review, 41: 133–151.

Fischer, C. S. (1982). *To dwell among friends: Personal networks in town and city*. Chicago: University of Chicago Press.

Francis, P. A. (1991, May). *Poverty in Bangladesh: Profile and policy implications*. Report prepared for the Overseas Development Administration.
Friedman, J. (1996). Rethinking poverty: Empowerment and citizen's rights. *International Social Science Journal, 148*(June), 161–171.
Gibbs, J. P. (1961). *Urban research methods*. Princeton, NJ: D. Van Nostrand Company.
Glaeser, E. L. (2013). *A world of cities: The causes and consequences of urbanization in poorer countries*. National Bureau of Economic Research Working Paper Np. 19745, Cambridge. Retrieved May 30, 2019, from https://www.nber.org/papers/w19745.pdf.
Glaeser, E. L., & Gottlieb, J. D. (2009). The wealth of cities: Agglomeration economies and spatial equilibrium in the United States. *Journal of Economic Literature, 47*(4), 983–1028.
Gold, K. L. (2006). Youth economic empowerment as poverty reduction strategy in Ilorin Metropolis. *Journal of Women in Colleges of Education (JOWICE), 10*, 281–287.
Guest, A. M., Cover, J. K., Matsueda, R. L., & Kubrin, C. E. (2006). Neighbourhood context and neighbouring ties. *City & Community, 5*(4), 363–385.
Hauser, P. M., and Duncan, 0. D. (Eds.) (1959). The study of population: An inventory and appraisal, Chicago: University of Chicago Press.
Henderson, J. V. (2010). Cities and development. *Journal of Regional Science, 50*(1), 515–540.
Idriss, J., Alamgir, M., & Panuccio, T. (1992). *The state of world rural poverty*. London: IT Publications.
Islam, N., Huda, Narayan, F. B., & Rana, P. B. (1997). Addressing the urban poverty agenda in Bangladesh. Dhaka: University Press Limited.
Jackson, D. (1972). *Poverty*. London: Macmillan &.
Jedwab, R., & Vollrath, D. (2015). Urbanization without growth in historical perspective. *Explorations in Economic History, 58*, 1–21.
Jefferson, M. (1909). The anthropogeography of some great cities. *Bulletin of American Geographical Society, XLI*, 537–660.
Jones, G. A. (Ed.). (2003). *Urban land markets in transition*. CD ROM. Cambridge, MA: Lincoln Institute of Land Policy.
Kemp, R. (1994). Technology and the transition to environmental sustainability: The problem of technological regime shifts. *Futures, 26*(10), 1023–1046.
Lewis, O. (1958). Village life in Northern India. Urban, ILO: University of Illinois Press.
Lipton, M. (1977). Why poor people stay poor: A study of urban bias in world development. London: Temple Smith.
McGranahan, G., & Martine, G. (Eds.). (2014). *Urban growth in emerging economies: Lessons from the BRICS*. Abingdon: Routledge.
McGranahan, G., Satterthwaite, D. (2014). *Urbanisation: Concepts and trends*. Working Paper, International Institute for Environment and Development, London.

Michaels, G., Rauch, F., & Redding, S. J. (2012). Urbanization and structural transformation. *The Quarterly Journal of Economics, 127*(2), 535–586.
Miller, J. E., & Korenman, S. (1994). Poverty and children's nutritional status in the United States. *American Journal of Epidemiology, 140*(3), 233–243.
Mooya, M. M., & Chris, E. C. (2007). Informal urban property markets and poverty alleviation: A conceptual framework, *Urban Studies, 44*(1): 147–165.
Morris, M. D. (1979). *Measuring the condition of the world's poor: The physical quality of life index*. London: Frank Cass.
Moser, C. (1995). Women, gender and urban development policy: Challenges for current and future research. *Third World Planning Review, 17*(2), 223–237.
Murray, C. (1984). *Losing ground*. New York: Harper Collins.
Narayan, D., Chambers, R., Shah, M., & Petesch, P. (2000). *Voices of the poor: Crying out for change*. New York: Oxford University Press for the World Bank.
Offiong, D. A. (2001). *Globalization: Post-neodependency and poverty in Africa*. Enugu: Fourth Dimension Publishing Co.
Ojha, P. D. (1970). A configuration of Indian poverty: Inequality and levels of living. *Reserve Bank of India Bulletin, 24*(1):16–27.
Oppenheim, C., & Harker, L. (1996). *Poverty: The facts*. London: Child Poverty Action Group.
Petmesidou, M., & Tsoulouvis, L. (1994). Aspects of the changing political economy of Europe: Welfare state, class segmentation and planning in the postmodern era. *Sociology, 28*(2), 499–519.
Pigou, A. C. (1952). *Employment policy: Essays in economics*. London: Macmillan.
Queen, S., & Carpenter, D. (1953). *The American city* (p. 265). New York: McGraw-Hill.
Ringen, S. (1988). Direct and indirect measures of poverty. *Journal of Social Policy, 17*(3), 351–365.
Santarelli, E., & Figini, P. (2002). *Does globalisation reduce poverty? Some empirical evidence for the developing countries*. Working Papers 459, Dipartimento Scienze Economiche, Universita' di Bologna.
Satterthwaite, D. (1995). The under-estimation and misrepresentation of urban poverty. *Environment and Urbanization, 7*(1), 3–10.
Satterthwaite, G., McGranahan, G., & Tacoli, C. (2010). Urbanization and its implications for food and farming. *Phil. Trans. R. Soc., 365*, 2809–2820.
Seebohm, R. B. (1901). *Poverty: A study of town life*. London: Palgrave Macmillan.
Sen, A. K. (1981). *Poverty and famines: An essay on entitlement and deprivation*. Oxford: Clarendon Press.
Sen, A. K. (1984). *Resources, values, and development*. Cambridge. MA: Harvard University Press.
Sen, A. K. (1999). *Development as freedom*. Oxford: Oxford University Press.
Silva, K. T., & Athukorala, K. (1996). South Asia: An overview. In Yen, E. Samad, S. A. and Miller, S. M. (Eds.) Poverty: A global Review. Hand book as Poverty Research. Oslo and Paris: Scandinavian University press (pp. 65–85).

Sorokin, P., & Zimmerman, C. C. (1929). *Principles of rural-urban sociology* (p. xv). New York: Henry Holt and Co.
Tacoli, C. (2017). Migration and inclusive urbanization. Population Division. Department of Economics and Social Affairs. United Nations Secretariat. New York: United Nations.
Tacoli, C., & Agergaard, J. (2017). *Urbanisation, rural transformations and food systems: The role of small towns.* Human Settlements Working Paper. IIED, London.
Tacoli, C., McGranahan, C., & Satterthwaite, D. (2014). *Urbanization, rural-urban mingartion and urban poverty.* World Migration Report, 2015. A Background Report. International Organization for Migration (IOM).
Thompson, W. (1935). *Population problems.* New York: McGraw Hill Book Co.
Todaro, M. P. (1994). *Economic development* (5th ed.). New York, London: Longman.
Townsend, P. (1979). *Poverty in the United Kingdom: A survey of household resources and standards of living.* Harmondsworth: Penguin Books.
U.S. Bureau of Census. (2002). *Urban and rural definitions.* Retrieved September 23, 2017, from http://www.census.gov/population/censusdata/urdef.txt.
United Cities and Local Governments (UCLG). (2016). *Co-creating the urban future: the agenda of metropolises, cities and territories.* Fourth Global Report on Local Democracy and Decentralization, UCLG, Barcelona.
United Nations. (2012). *World urbanization prospects: The 2011 revision.* New York: Department of Economic and Social Affairs, Population Division.
United Nations Human Settlements Programme (UNHabitat). (2003). Expert group meeting on urban indicators. Secure Tenure, Slums and Global Sample of Cities, October 28–30, 2002, Revised Draft Report (P.33).
Wilcox, W. F. (1926). A definition of city in terms of pousity. In E. W. Burgess (Ed.), *The urban community: Selected papers from the proceedings of the American Sociological Society*, 1925. Chicago: University of Chicago Press.
Wilson, W. J. (1987). *The truly disadvantaged.* Chicago: The University of Chicago Press.
Wilson, W. J. (1996). *When work disappears: The world of the new urban poor.* New York: Knopf.
Wirth, L. (1938). Urbanism as a way of life. *The American Journal of Sociology, 44*(1), 1–24.
World Bank. (1991). *Urban policy and economic development: An agenda for the 1990s.* World Bank Policy Paper, Washington, DC.
World Bank. (2001). *Land, security, property rights and the urban poor: Twenty five years of World Bank experience.* World Bank Briefing Note 8.
Wratten, E. (1995). Conceptualizing urban poverty. *Environment and Urbanization, 7*(1), 11–33.

CHAPTER 3

Urbanization and Urban Poverty in Bangladesh

Introduction

Urbanization and growth are two inseparable elements of a country's development. There is hardly any country in the world that has attained the status of the middle-income country without making a substantial population transformation in urban areas. Thus, the process of sustainable growth in developing countries requires a moderate rate of urbanization. Of course, urbanization offers different types of benefits to the people of the country (Annez and Buckley 2009) by providing better living standards in the form of higher life expectancy, higher levels of literacy, better provision of water and sanitation and other related services. Moreover, it creates scope for accommodating economic activities and large population that could ensure better environmental sustainability within the concentration of urban settlements (World Bank 2009). At the same time, the process of urbanization has presented various challenges to policy-makers and the populace at large. Thus, it is not always welcomed, as management of urbanization that requires nurturing growth can be costly. Urbanization thus stands at the crossroads of the study of development and growth. Although it is considered a necessary prerequisite of multidimensional structural transformation of many low-income societies, it does impose a burden on governments in terms of its management (Annez and Buckley 2009). On the other hand, the rapid transformation of the World's population in urban areas has been facilitating the growth of poverty in cities and towns. The concentration of rapid urbanization in the Global South

P. K. Panday, *The Face of Urbanization and Urban Poverty in Bangladesh*, https://doi.org/10.1007/978-981-15-3332-7_3

is one of the prime factors to have affected the growth of urban poverty in some countries at a higher rate than rural poverty (UNFPA 2007). Such growth has been compelling urban residents to become dependent on cash incomes to fulfill their basic needs (Beall and Fox 2007). Higher prices of goods and services in urban areas have affected the livelihood of the people in rural areas, as they too are forced to pay higher prices for goods and services (Banerjee and Duflo 2007). Thus, one may assume that there seems to be a strong interrelationship between urbanization and urban poverty. Under this circumstance, the main thrust of this chapter is to portray the different dimensions of urbanization and urban poverty in the context of Bangladesh.

History and the Present State of Urbanization in Bangladesh

The urbanization process in Bangladesh began at a slow pace, and gained momentum. During the early twentieth century (about 1901), the total population residing in urban areas of Bangladesh under British India, comprised only 2.43% (or about 0.7 million). The rate of urban population growth reached nearly 4% in 1941 with a total population of 2.54 million residing in the urban areas. However, the process of urbanization found momentum after its partition from the Indian subcontinent in 1947, when the present Bangladesh became erstwhile East Pakistan. Since then, there has been a steady and positive change in the growth of urban population, and number of urban centers in the country (Islam 2012). The growing urban population reached about 2.64 million in 1961 from 1.83 million in 1951. But, what triggered this boom during this phase? The "migration" of a vast majority of Muslims, residents of urban areas, from India post partition in 1947 (Hossain 2008). This growth was also facilitated by the emergence and expansion of new centers of trade, commerce, industry, and the government administration that acted as pull factors for many people to migrate from rural to urban areas post 1947 (Ahmed 1968).

A prodigious growth was observed from 1947 to 1961 in the process of urbanization; the rate of urbanization rose to 137.6% with a yearly increase of 6.7% as opposed to 3.7% of the previous decade. Most importantly, the nature of urbanization remained the same, as in the British period. It is important to mention here that in the pre-partition period, the government did not implement large-scale industrial development plans in East Pakistan (now Bangladesh), considering it as their colony (CUS 1976).

The process of urbanization continued its growth trajectory from 1961 to 1974. During this time, the number of urban population rose to 6 million, comprising around 8.0% of the total population. Later, the total number of urban population increased from 8.9% in 1974 to 15.5% in 1981. Interestingly, from 1974 to 1981, the rate of inter-censal change was at 110.7%, a yearly increase of 10%. This growth was mostly facilitated by the intrusion of rural people in cities (Hossain 2008). Besides, a couple of other factors also influenced the influx of rural people into cities; they include the post-liberation war, economic penury and the negative impact of environmental disasters (Islam 2012).

One important dimension of the growth of urban population from 1981 to 1991 was the extended definition of urban places where the newly created 460 Upazila headquarters were included as urban areas. This led to a 30% increase in the urban population. Notably, the government's decision to include the Upazila headquarters was a reflection of the role of the politico-administrative decision-making, which, in turn, helped in determining the demographic status of a region as urban instead of considering the quality of urbanism. The next ten years (i.e. 1991–2001) produced a relatively slow growth in terms of increase in the urban population, at a rate of 5.4%. Nevertheless, the growth by and large was steady, whereby the number of urban population rose to 28.61 million in 2001 (Panday 2017), almost doubling to 42.7 million in 2011. If one were to compare the increase of urban population from 1974 to 2011, one would note that there has been a 6.8 times growth within a span 37 years, while the increase in ratio would be about 1.7 times in the rural areas alone (Islam 2015). The following table (Table 3.1) shows the trend of urbanization in Bangladesh during 1901–2011.

From the Table 3.1, a huge difference is evident between the exponential growth rate of the urban and rural population. If we compare the growth rate of urban and rural population during 1974–2011, it is evident that the rate of urban population growth was 5.18% as opposed to 1.36% for the rural population. On the other hand, the country has observed only 2.8% growth for the total population during this time. Thus, the rapid growth of urban population has transformed a rural country into an urbanized country (Panday 2017).

Table 3.1 Trends of urbanization in Bangladesh (1901–2011)

Year	*Urban population (in million)*	*Rural population (in million)*	*Percentage urban*	*Urban annual exponential growth rate (%)*	*Rural annual exponential growth rate (%)*	*Urban–rural growth differential (AEGR)*
1901	0.70	28.23	2.43	–	–	–
1911	0.81	30.75	2.56	1.39	0.86	0.54
1921	0.88	32.38	2.64	0.85	0.52	0.33
1931	1.07	34.53	3.02	2.00	0.64	1.36
1941	1.54	40.46	3.66	3.59	1.58	2.01
1951	1.82	40.24	4.33	1.69	−0.05	1.74
1961	2.64	48.20	5.19	3.72	1.80	1.92
1974	6.27	65.21	8.78	6.66	2.32	4.33
1981	13.54	73.58	15.54	10.99	1.73	9.26
1991	22.46	89.00	20.15	5.06	1.90	3.16
2001	28.61	95.25	23.10	2.42	0.68	1.74
2011	42.70	107.80	28.37	4.01	1.24	2.77
2020 (Projected)	52.2	123.2	37.7	–	–	–
2030 (Projected)	98.6	124.1	44.3	–	–	–

Source: Islam (2015) and Rahman (2014)

Urban Growth and Its Impact on the National Economy

The economy of Bangladesh has experienced a structural change in the last decade. The pattern of urbanization has indeed played an important role in the process of accelerating the economic development of the country. Thus, it is quite impossible to separate urbanization and economic development from one another. Importantly, the country's economy in recent times has connected to the world market through the globalization process, which in turn has created a favorable investment climate, while establishing good governance. Now, it would be easier for the country to use the benefits of functional urbanization for making visible economic advancements in the future (Hasnath 2012). UN-HABITAT (2010) stated that individuals could earn higher incomes in a country when the growth rate of urbanization is high, as there is an accumulation in terms of the income level. This is the reason for higher-income countries to be characterized by their high GDP numbers, and higher levels of urbanization thereof (Cited in Kawsar 2012). It may therefore be assumed that the per capita GDP and the level of urbanization do have a strong interrelationship, presented through Table 3.2 from a global perspective.

Table 3.2 delineates ten countries that have been ranked in terms of their GDP numbers, as well as their higher rate of urbanization (above 20%), with Brunei being the exception (63.2%). Herein, it is important to note that like other developed countries, urbanization and economic development are positively correlated for Bangladesh also. Over a period of time, the share of the urban sector to Bangladesh's GDP has been on the rise. For instance, the contribution of the urban sector in terms of GDP was 43% in 2001, as compared to 25.36% from 1972 to 1993. Additionally, it is worth noting that the country's status as a rural agrarian economy has been outstripped by the hasty growth of urbanization. This, in fact, has negatively affected the contribution of the rural economy to the GDP at a reduced rate of 57% in 2000–2001, as compared to 74.64% in 1972–1973 (Panday 2017). On the other hand, due to the influence of rapid growth of urbanization and increasing GDP, the regional income disparity has been amplified, whereby the rate of inequality in the monthly average household income in urban and rural areas has increased. For instance, the contribution of the urban sector in GDP in monthly average income between rural and urban rose to 71.64% of rural income in 2005,

Table 3.2 GDP per capita of top 10 countries along with their level of urbanization (2018)

Rank No.	*Country*	*GDP 2018 (US$) (Round figure)*	*Level of urbanization (%) (2018)*
1	Qatar	130,475	99.1
2	Luxembourg	106,705	91
3	Singapore	100,345	100
4	Brunei	79,530	77.6
5	Ireland	78,785	63.2
6	Norway	74,356	82.2
7	United Arab Emirates	69,382	86.5
8	Kuwait	67,000	100
9	Switzerland	64,649	73.8
10	USA	62,606	82.3

Source: World Economic Outlook Database (2019) and World Factbook Urbanization (2019)

Table 3.3 Household rural–urban income inequality in Bangladesh (in TK)

Survey year	*Monthly average household income in residence*				
	National	*Urban*	*Rural*	*Difference between urban and rural income*	*The difference as a percent of rural income (%)*
1991–1992	3341	4832	3109	1723	55
1995–1996	4366	7973	3658	4315	117.96
2000	5842	9878	4816	5062	105
2005	7203	9878	6096	4367	71.64
2010	11,479	16475	9648	6829	70.78
2016	15945	22565	13353	9212	68.99

Source: HIES (2016) and Government of Bangladesh (2010): 205–206

70.78% in 2010 and 68.99% in 2010 as compared to 55% in 1991–1992 (Kawsar 2012). Most surprisingly, the rate of income inequality was 117.96% and 106% in 1995–1996 and 2000, respectively (Table 3.3). This was because the growth of urbanization was at the peak during this time.

The discussion above leads us to conclude that urbanization does positively contribute to national economic development. However, there are certain areas where urbanization also negatively affects the economic growth; for instance, the impact of urbanization on the unequal income gap between the rural and urban households as shown in the earlier paragraph. Thus, the relationship between these two cannot always be analyzed in a straight line. It is due to this indirect relationship that Bangladesh has found it difficult to capitalize on an optimal accumulation and slipover benefit of the urbanization process at large. Add to that the nonexistence of an all-inclusive development policy plan to deal with the urbanization process, coupled with several negative externalities (e.g. urban cramming, environmental pollution, inadvertent urban growth, and flared income inequality) have been affecting the growth trajectory of the country (Panday 2017). Therefore, in order to improve, the government should initiate institutional reforms, create provisions for serviced land, and intensify an own-source of revenue for urban bodies.

The Situation of Urban Poverty in Bangladesh

Going by what we have discussed so far, one cannot deny the importance of urbanization as a key growth driver and consequent poverty reduction. But, it is also true that the process of urbanization at large has failed to significantly contribute to the urban poverty reduction process, despite having significantly reduced national poverty in different parts of the world (Cohen 2001; Ravallion et al. 2007).

The recent development dynamics of Bangladesh has been influenced greatly by the rapid growth of urbanization. In 2018, Bangladesh's urban population constituted 36.5% of the total population of the country. This changing dynamics did to a great extent reduce the rate of rural poverty (Table 3.4), while giving a raise to the issue of urban poverty. In fact, in the last decade, urban poverty has possibly been the greatest distinguishing characteristic of the cities in Bangladesh. The World Bank (2007) in its report stated that there is a festering or actively worsening situation of human development in the country, which is worrisome indeed.

One of the important dimensions is that these large numbers of urban poor are required to live in illegal settlements in different parts of the cities. They fail to have access even to adequate and safe housing and to land and basic services; they suffer from deprivation and fail to participate in the political process and live with the threat of eviction. This situation predominantly exists in large city corporations where most of the urban

Table 3.4 Poverty trends in Bangladesh (calculated based on upper poverty line)

Year	*National (%)*	*Urban (%)*	*Rural (%)*	*Poverty gap (%)*	*Squared poverty gap (%)*
1983/1984	52.3	40.9	53.8	15.0	5.9
1988/1989	47.8	35.9	49.7	13.1	4.8
1991/1992	49.7	33.6	52.9	14.6	5.6
1995/1996	53.1	35.0	56.7	15.5	5.7
2000	49.8	36.6	53.1	13.8	4.8
2005	40.0	28.4	43.8	9	2.9
2010	31.5	21.3	35.2	6.5	2.0
2016	24.3	N/A	N/A	6.5	1.5

Source: Azam and Imai (2009) and HIES (2016)

poor tend to live in low-income settlements, commonly known as *bastee* or slum. According to the census report of 2014, 60.43% of slum dwellers and floating population lived there. The report also stated that of a total of 13,943 slums all over the country, 65.40% are located with the city corporation (i.e. 1639 in Dhaka (North), 1755 in Dhaka (South), 2216 in Chittagong, 1258 in Gazipur, 1134 in Khulna, 671 in Sylhet, 137 in Barisal, 104 in Rajshahi, 49 in Rangpur, 41 in Comilla and 82 in Narayanganj). Table 3.5 shows the distribution of slums by locality (City Corporation, Municipalities and Other Urban Areas).

Although urban poverty remains one of the greatest challenges for governments of developing countries, there is still a lack of political will and commitment of the governments to deal with the issue (Banks et al. 2011). Specifically, the Bangladesh government has almost disregarded the issue of urban poverty, while figuring out their strategies to deal with poverty since 1971. This is evident through urban poverty's exclusion from the first draft of the Poverty Reduction Strategy Paper (PRSP), which is one of the most important policy documents, as regards poverty reduction.

Table 3.5 Distribution of slums by locality (City Corporation, Municipalities and Other Urban Areas)

Locality	*Slum census 2014*		*Slum census 1997*	
	Number	*Percentage*	*Number*	*Percentage*
Barisal	137	0.98	NA	NA
Chittagong	2216	15.90	186	6.22
Camilla	41	0.29	NA	NA
Dhaka (North)	1639	11.76	1579[a]	52.79
Dhaka (South)	1755	12.59		
Gazipur	1285	9.22	NA	NA
Khulna	1134	8.14	202	6.75
Narayanganj	82	0.59	NA	NA
Rajshahi	104	0.75	84	2.81
Rangpur	49	0.35	NA	NA
Sylhet	671	4.82	NA	NA
City Corporation Total	*9113*	*65.40*	*NA*	*NA*
Municipalities	3357	24.04	940	31.43
Other urban areas	1465	10.51	NA	NA
National	*13935*	*100*	*2991*	*100*

Source: Census of Slum Areas and Floating Populations (2014)

[a]During this time Dhaka was not divided into two city corporations

Initially, the PRSP was rural poverty-driven; urban poverty was included in the final draft due to pressure from different stakeholders. Unfortunately, the half-page summary did not clearly specify the vulnerability of the urban poor. Importantly, it did not enlist the strategies that were required to deal with the issue (Banks et al. 2011). Since the issue did not get adequate attention in the government's most significant policy documents for poverty reduction, there is hardly any policy to deal with urban poverty, with no government money earmarked for these people (Banks 2008).

Another dimension of urban poverty is the branding of the urban poor. The issue has remained a neglected area at the policy level because people living in slums have been perceived as scoundrels or even criminals, as opposed to the people living in rural areas, who are perceived as epitomizing "social harmony". Due to this erroneous perception, the government tends to go after them, looking to evict them, rather than assisting them to improve their livelihoods. However, in recent times, there has been a gradual change in the government's perception, due to which some attempts are being made for poverty reduction in these areas (i.e. urban slums). The government, along with international and national organizations, has begun investing resources for improving the livelihoods of the *bastees*. For instance, the "Urban Sector", a local Consultative Group, was made functional under the chairmanship of GIZ in 2008, where the decision was taken to shift the focus from infrastructure to social development and urban poverty. The group started working on improving the profile of the urban poor, and published a document "Bridging the Urban Divide in Bangladesh", which is considered as a strategic approach to poverty reduction (LCG 2010). The government also incorporated "urban development" in the second National Strategy for Accelerated Poverty Reduction NSAPR (2009–2011). Of course, this does not guarantee that the urban poor would receive the benefit of urban development and growth (LGD 2010). From the donor's perspective, one of the largest initiatives was undertaken by UNDP by implementing the Urban Partnership for Poverty Reduction (UPPR) project with financial support from DFID and UN-HABITAT and in partnership with the Local Government Engineering Department (LGED) of Bangladesh Government (Banks 2011). Like UNDP, many donors have been implementing programs on urban poverty, which will be discussed in the next three chapters.

Rural–Urban Linkage

In order to comprehend urbanization and urban poverty clearly, it is important to understand the urban–rural linkage, as the interdependence of social, economic and environmental development between rural and urban areas is widely recognized worldwide. In the context of Bangladesh, the process of rural development is strongly influenced by city corporations and secondary cities, as these serve as the prime markets for goods and products produced at the rural level (Mazed 2003). Importantly, they also provide working opportunities for the daily-wage labor coming from rural areas. Urban areas therefore have a strong dependency on rural areas, as the latter ensure the supply of food, labor, raw materials for manufacturing, and markets for their products. This sort of interdependency plays an important role in the development of rural and urban areas. The physical propinquity to the neighboring countryside has strengthened their linkage in the context of secondary cities and towns (UN-HABITAT 2007). These tiny cities have emerged as centers of trade and places for carrying out social and economic activities. Further, these cities have turned into prominent centers of service delivery for the rural neighborhood, as they create opportunities for the rural people to visit towns for accessing public services without much difficulty, as compared to municipal cities where they tend to suffer while they opt to get access to service there. On the other hand, the rural population could use the benefits of schools and other facilities that accelerate the development of rural areas (Satterthwaite 2002).

In addition to these economic benefits, the linkage could contribute a lot in the process of rural–urban development by creating long-term job opportunities for the people who are migrating from rural to urban areas. Remittances that are being sent by the relatives of the rural people working in the urban areas are helping them not only to lead a better life in the rural areas, but also to cope with different seasonal challenges in the form of *Monga*, and environmental upheavals. Additionally, the migration of the rural populace could also serve as a source of cheap labor for cities. The importance of rural–urban linkage to the urban poor is also considerable, as they invariably tend to suffer from food insecurity; thus, many of them fall under the "direct calorie intake" poverty line. The rise of food price globally has pushed these people in a vulnerable position in a country like Bangladesh. This has made them even more dependent on rural areas for the supply of food in cities. Thus, in order to deal with the issue of food insecurity as well as maximum utilization of the potential of the rural–urban linkages, more attention is required in strengthening this linkage (GoB 2010).

Conclusion

The changing nature of urban poverty in the Global South has made governments of developing countries, planners and researchers think about shifting their priorities while developing strategies for poverty reduction. Herein, it is important to note that the process of urbanization does have a strong relationship with a nation's economy. For instance, top countries that have the highest per capita GDP in the world do have a high rate of urbanization.

This chapter has emphasized that Bangladesh has been experiencing a high degree of growth in terms of urbanization and urban population. The process of urbanization has been contributing to the national economy greatly. But, the increasing numbers of urban poor are living a substandard life in slums without having access to basic services. Most, importantly, governments, especially of developing nations, have tended to overlook the issue of urban poverty in their poverty reduction strategies. However, over a period of time, an attempt has been made to address the issue, whereby the government and development partners have come together, both at the national and international levels. The policy-makers have at last understood that the contribution of urbanization to a nation's economy would decrease if the situation of the urban poor does not improve. The next chapter sheds light on slum formation and slum-upgrading initiatives in Bangladesh.

References

Ahmed, N. (1968). *An economic geography of East Pakistan*. London: Oxford University Press.

Annez, P. C., & Buckley, R. M. (2009). Urbanization and growth: Setting the context. In M. Spence, P. C. Annez, & R. M. Buckley (Eds.), *Urbanization and growth*. A report prepared for the Commission on Growth and Development, The International Bank for Reconstruction and Development, the World Bank.

Azam, M. S., & Imai, K. S. (2009). Vulnerability and poverty in Bangladesh. *ASARC Working Paper No. 2009/02*. Retrieved May 24, 2019, from https://cnnd.crawford.anu.edu.au/acde/asarc/pdf/papers/2009/WP2009_02.pdf.

Banerjee, A. V., & Duflo, E. (2007). The economic lives of the poor. *Journal of Economic Perspective, 21*(1), 41–167.

Banks, N. (2008). A tale of two wards: Political participation and the urban poor in Dhaka city. *Environment and Urbanization, 20*(2), 361–376.

Banks, N. (2011). Improving donor support for urban poverty reduction: A focus on South Asia. *UNU-WIDER Working Paper No. 2011/68*. Helsinki: United Nations University.

Banks, N., Roy, M., & Hulme, D. (2011). Neglecting the urban poor in Bangladesh: Research, policy and action in the context of climate change. *Environment and Urbanization, 23*(2), 487–502.

Beall, J., & Fox, S. (2007). Urban poverty and development in the 21st century: Towards an inclusive and sustainable world. *Oxfam GB Research Report*. Oxford: Oxfam.

Census of Slum Areas and Floating Populations. (2014). Bangladesh Bureau of Statistics, Statistics and Information Division, Ministry of Planning. Dhaka: Government of Bangladesh.

Centre for Urban Studies (CUS). (1976). Squatters in Bangladesh cities: A survey of urban squatters in Dhaka, Chittagong and Khulna–1974. Dhaka.

Cohen, M. (2001). The impact of the global economy on cities. In M. Freire & R. Stren (Eds.), *The challenge of urban government: Policies and practices*. Washington, DC: The World Bank.

Government of Bangladesh. (2010). *Bridging the urban divide in Bangladesh*. Event Report for the Joint Conversation Event of the Local Government, Ministry of Local Government, Rural Development and Cooperatives and the LGD Working Group Urban Sector, Bangladesh. Dhaka.

Hasnath, S. A. (2012). Urban future in South Asia. In A. Nazam & M. Yusuf (Eds.), *South Asia 2060*. London: Anthem.

Hossain, S. (2008). Rapid urban growth and poverty in Dhaka City. *Bangladesh E-Journal of Sociology, 5*(1), 1–24.

Household Income and Expenditure Survey (HIES). (2016). Bangladesh Bureau of Statistics, Statistics and Information Division, Ministry of Planning. Dhaka: Government of Bangladesh.

Islam, N. (2012). *Urbanization and urban governance in Bangladesh*. A background paper prepared for the 13th Annual Global Development Conference on "Urbanization and Development: Delving Deeper into the Nexus", June 16–18, Budapest.

Islam, N. (2015). *Urbanization in Bangladesh: Challenges and opportunities*. A paper presented in the Conference on Towards Sustained Eradication of Extreme Poverty in Bangladesh, Organized by General Economics Decision of the Planning Commission in Collaboration with Bangladesh Bank and Bangladesh Institute of Development Studies, Held on 8–9 April 2015. Dhaka: NEC Conference Room, Planning Commission.

Kawsar, M. A. (2012). Urbanization, economic development and inequality. *Bangladesh Research Publications Journal, 6*(4), 440–448.

Local Consultative Group Urban Sector (LCG). (2010). *Bridging the urban divide in Bangladesh*. Dhaka: GTZ and LCG, Dhaka.

Local Government Division (LGD) (2010). Bridging the urban divide in Bangladesh: Towards a strategic approach to urban poverty reduction. Dhaka: Government of Bangladesh.

Mazed, M. A. (2003). *Post-harvest technology for employment generation in rural Bangladesh*. A paper presented at UNAPCAEM (Asian and Pacific Centre for Agricultural Engineering and Machinery of United Nations ESCAP) Regional Seminar on Post-Harvest Technology for Major Crops. Kunming, Yunnan Province, November 3–5, China.

Panday, P. K. (2017). *Reforming urban governance: The city corporation*. UK: Palgrave Macmillan. London.

Rahman, H. Z. (2014). *Urbanization in Bangladesh: Challenges and priorities*. A paper presented at the First Bangladesh Economists' Forum's Conference, Held on 21–22 June. Dhaka: Radisson Blu Water Garden Hotel.

Ravallion, M., Chen, S., & Sangraula, P. (2007). New evidence on the urbanization of global poverty. *World Bank Policy Research Working Paper Series 4199*. Washington, DC: The World Bank.

Satterthwaite, D. (2002). *Coping with rapid urban growth*. RICS International Paper Series. London: Royal Institution of Chartered Surveyors.

UNFPA. (2007). State of the world population-2007: Unleashing the potential of urban growth. New York: United Nations Population Fund.

UN-HABITAT. (2007). *Global report of human settlements 2007: Enhancing urban safety and security*. Nairobi: UN-HABITAT.

UN-HABITAT Annual Report. (2010). Nairobi: United Nations Human Settlements Programme (UN-HABITAT).

World Bank. (2007). To the MDGs and beyond: Accountability and institutional innovation in Bangladesh. *Bangladesh Development Series No. 14*. Dhaka: The World Bank.

World Bank. (2009). *World development report 2009: Reshaping economic geography*. Washington, DC: The World Bank.

World Economic Outlook Database. (2019). International Monetary Fund. Database updated in April. Retrieved June 7, 2019, from https://www.imf.org/external/pubs/ft/weo/2019/01/weodata/index.aspx.

World Factbook Urbanization. (2019). Central Intelligence Agency. Retrieved June 7, 2019, from https://www.cia.gov/library/publications/the-world-factbook/.

CHAPTER 4

Formation of Slums and Slums Upgrading Initiatives in Bangladesh

Introduction

From 2008 onward, the world witnessed an enormous growth in urban population. Most importantly, most of the populace, especially in developing countries began to live in urban slums. Among the developing countries, the most urbanized slum populace was witnessed in the sub-Saharan Africa region. Due to a phenomenal spike in growth of urban slum dwellers, the people of these regions had to face several challenges with regard to basic amenities, like scarcity of safe drinking water, safe sanitation, overcrowding and insufficient housing. Apart from the population burst in the sub-Saharan region, western, southern and eastern Asia also experienced a similar phenomenon. In fact, from 2001 to 2011, South Asia's urban population grew by 130 million people. It is expected that the number of urban population within this region would rise to almost 259 million in the next 15 years (Ellis and Roberts 2016). Northern Africa is possibly the only country that experienced an annual decrease of 0.15% in its population living in urban slums, which effectively helped in improving the quality of life (UN-DESA 2006). The stupendous rise in urban population has been creating enormous pressure on cities. Consequently, the people, who come in from rural areas for their livelihoods, do not have tenure of land, and they begin to reside wherever they find vacant. The main objective of this chapter is to discuss different causes of slum formation, and explain

P. K. Panday, *The Face of Urbanization and Urban Poverty in Bangladesh*, https://doi.org/10.1007/978-981-15-3332-7_4

diverse initiatives through which the situation of slums could be improved. Before shedding light on these discussions it is important to define what a slum is and who are living there.

Definition and Meaning of Slum

The term "slum" does not have any uniform meaning and definition. Instead, the term is used differently in diverse country-contexts. However, there are a few commonalities in the meaning and definition of a "slum" or "squatter" settlement. The first commonality is that slum is a residential area within an urban setting where a large number of extremely poor people without any land tenure barge in to live. "Slum" was first used in the 1820s to denote the poorest quality of housing, featured by lack of sanitary facilities. It was supposed to be the "den" of marginalized activities, including crimes and drug dealing. Notably, even to this day, this derogatory undertone of the term remains. Nevertheless, as regards its applicability in developing countries, the term is used to denote poor quality of housing (Ward 1976).

In terms of the dictionary meaning of the term, a slum denotes "*a squalid and overcrowded urban street or district inhabited by very poor people; a house or building unfit for human habitation*" (Oxford Dictionary of English). In line with this meaning, scholars in the earlier days defined the term as a congested and dirty place within industrialized cities (especially of Europe and North America) (Ward 1976; WSUP 2007). However, in 2007, a UN expert group defined the term as an area featured by insufficient access to safe water, poor access to sanitation and other infrastructure, poor structural quality of housing, congestion and insecure housing status (UN-HABITAT 2007).

Of late, urban poverty, especially in developing countries, has been manifested through these slums or informal settlements. Structurally, it may be situated on different types of building with well-maintained structures in some places. Largely, slums may be categorized into two broad types, that is, "slums of hope" and "slums of despair". While the former represents an upward trend that is new, with the experience of going through a process of development, consolidation and improvement, the latter represents a declining trend. Herein, the inhabitants are forced to experience vulnerable environmental conditions and quality of life (Camilo 2008). The discussion above leads us to draw an operational definition of the concept of slums as low-income settlements without proper access to clean water, sanitation facilities and insufficient living space that does not hand land tenure rights.

The Formation of Slums Globally

A slum is not a new phenomenon in development literature. It has remained an integral part of most cities of the world. The development and growth of slums have close linkages with the early days of urbanization, industrialization and urban population. As a concept, "slum" carries a lot of importance in urban areas, as the poor people of the cities solely depend on slums for their housing needs. Given the enormity of the importance of the term "slum", we present herewith a few factors that have been identified to be facilitating its growth in the urban areas, globally.

Population Growth and Urbanization

Different parts of the world have experienced rapid growth of urbanization due to natural growth and migration of a huge pool of people from the rural areas to the cities. Currently, most countries of the world have a large chunk of their populace residing in urban areas. A revised version of the UN World Urbanization Prospects report that was published in 2014 stated that the ratio of the world's population living in urban areas in 2014 was 54%, having grown from about 13% in 1990, and 49% in 2005. The report had also predicted that by 2030, the ratio of world's population residing in cities would be 60%, and would increase by about another 6% by 2050. In other words, one-third of the world's population would be living in urban areas by 2050. As regards the overall count of the urban population, it was 3.9 billion in 2014 as compared to only 746 million in 1950 (United Nations 2014).

A closer look at the level and intensity of urbanization in terms of geographical locations suggests that the ratio of people living in urban areas of North American countries was 82% in 2014, while the ratio was 80% in Latin America and 73% each in the Caribbean countries and Europe, respectively. From a comparative perspective, the rate of urbanization in Africa and Asia is relatively low, as the population rate living in urban areas in these two regions were 40% and 48%, respectively, in 2014 (United

Nations 2014). Due to growing urbanization, cities have been facing numerous problems in meeting the housing needs of the poor, who do not even have the capacity to afford the cost of housing. These brutal realities force them to search for vacant places for living, which ultimately turn into slums in course of time.

Hasty Rural–Urban Migration

Since 1959, developing countries have been experiencing a steady decline in the number of people working in the agriculture sector. One of the prime factors that have contributed to this decline is the people's intention to maximize economic opportunities, and enjoy modern amenities of life in cities. However, there have been cases where rural people were compelled to move to cities post natural calamities, in search of their livelihood. This limitless influx of the rural populace into cities has not only been accelerating the expansion of urban slums, but has also been posing challenges related to housing, and meeting up with the basic necessities of life, like clean and adequate water supply, sanitation facilities, etc. Apart from these essential problems of basic existence, some other plaguing issues include transport, education, medical and recreation facilities, along with sufficient employment generation. Nevertheless, this spurt of informal settlements and squatters has also created opportunities for the informal sector, which has been meeting the needs of the urban poor by providing goods and services. For instance, the informal sector in sub-Saharan Africa provides about 72% of nonagricultural employment. Academicians and experts expect that of the total number of jobs created in the urban areas within the next few decades, 90% would be from the informal sector in the form of small-scale enterprises. Interestingly, this is going to happen in a time when there would be hardly any increase in the formal urban labor market, as the market has been shrinking in most developing countries.

Herein, it is noteworthy to state that the increase of migration from rural to urban areas has been extended beyond Africa, whereby Latin America and Asia have also experienced incredible growth. For instance, in the past 50 years, Latin America's urbanization growth rate has crossed 80%. Asia is not far behind; most of the Asian people (about 50%) live in urban areas. Major Asian cities including Mumbai, Kolkata, Bangkok, and Dhaka carry over 15 million people; among these, one-third live in urban slums (ADB 2014). A discussion of a few factors that have compelled people to migrate from rural to urban areas follows.

Migration Led by Push and Pull Factors

Different types of natural disasters along with continued ecological changes have forced many people to migrate to cities leaving their rural places of origin. For instance, cyclones like *Sidr* and *Aila* that hit coastal districts of Bangladesh, including Khulna and Sathkhira in 2007 and 2009, respectively, compelled several thousands of people to leave their rural homes to move to cities, as they had lost their homes and agricultural lands. On the other hand, different factors, including attraction for better life, availability of jobs, better education, better medical facilities, and openness in terms of lifestyle have pulled many more to the cities.

People's Understanding of the Attraction of Cities

In most cases, the migrants leave their rural homes intentionally to live in cities with the expectation that they would be able to enjoy the modern amenities of life in the form of improved transportation, better health opportunities and education, among others. Most importantly, they network with earlier migrants, due to which they become more informed of both the positive and negative aspects of city life.

Migration as a Survival Strategy for the Poorest

People migrate also in search for employment opportunities. Their expectation is that they could earn their livelihoods from diverse sources, which in turn would help them overcome their susceptibility to financial depressions.

Lucrative Working Opportunities

Job opportunities are quite high in urban areas as compared to rural areas. Thus, these opportunities attract the rural populace, who spend most of their lives in hardship without income and work. In turn, this has been influencing the upward social mobility toward cities, which has been stretching the cities to the brim on all fronts.

Displacement of People Due to Catastrophic Effect of Climate

Nowadays, climate change has become one of the most important push factors that compel people to leave their places of origin. Once these people are affected by different climatic disasters, they are distressed and too vulnerable even to fend for themselves for basic necessities like food, shelter, sanitation, etc. However, once they do migrate, most often they do not find any shelter. This forces them to put up just about anywhere, which gradually turns into urban slums over time.

The Decline of Incomes from Agriculture

When we talk about agriculture, it is well known that weather possibly affects this section the most, especially in terms of income. Additionally, due to the extensive use of fertilizers and pesticides these days, rural lands have been losing their fertility. On the other hand, agricultural lands have also been shrinking due to population growth. All these brutal realities have made rural people more vulnerable, and their search for better opportunities leads them to migrate to cities.

Political Struggle

The political struggle between contesting political groups has also become an influential factor that causes urban migration. In most cases, people who get involved in serious types of political conflict migrate to urban areas. However, at times, to save themselves from possible attacks of contending groups, people do migrate across borders. Some of the African countries are classic examples of migration across the border. Angola and Mozambique, for instance, are two African countries that have experienced a rapid growth of urbanization due to civil conflict. Although migration due to political struggles is not common in Bangladesh, there have been instances where people have migrated to urban areas, and in fact in some cases, even beyond borders. One of the dimensions of such migration is that the supporters of the opposition parties usually migrate to different places for fear of being harassed by the ruling party supporters and the law-enforcing agencies.

Hurried Industrialization Growth

The amplifying growth of commercial and industrial activities has opened up new demands for cheap labor in cities due to an acute shortage of adequate workforce. Initially, these job opportunities did encourage rural people to come to the cities in search of work. Over a period of time, this became a norm, whereby the people who could manage to get some work, subsequently brought their relatives along. Once they found work, they were compelled to look for shelter; however, due to their low-income levels, they found it difficult to afford decent shelter. Thus, they began building their own shelter wherever they possibly found empty places. Gradually, this catapulted into a large amalgamation of people, all living in close proximity, resulting thereby in "urban slums".

Lack of Good Urban Governance

Lack of good governance is also responsible for slums formation in cities. Having failed to recognize the rights of the urban poor, the government integrated these people into urban planning. Once they were integrated into the urban planning system, they began occupying other vacant places to build their shelters, thereby accelerating the growth of urban slums. Importantly, one needs to note that most governments do not have enough capacity to deal with different issues relating to the rapid growth of urbanization. The most worrying fact is that the rate of people coming in from rural to urban areas is much faster than the rate of incorporating them into the planning process.

Globalization and Slum Formation

There is a strong relationship between the process of slum formation, economic cycles, national income distribution trend, along with most important policies of national development. In the UNDP World Urbanization Prospects Report 2005, it was reported that the demand for skilled versus unskilled labor tends to increase manifold due to the cyclical nature of capitalism, along with the adverse impact of globalization. Effectively, this intensifies disparity and unequal distribution of new wealth, which possibly helped the process of slum formation in the first place. The report also noted that the renowned slums of different cities of the developed world were formed due to the global economic cycles (United Nations 2008).

The Response of the Government

The response and attitude of the government toward urbanization is another factor that contributes to the formation of slums in cities. Many governments tend to choose a "hostile approach" to urbanization with the belief that if urban services are made easily accessible to the slum dwellers, they would be lured into urban areas, which in turn would accelerate the growth of urban slums to a point beyond the government's control.

Finally, it can be said all the above factors have a direct relationship with poverty, which means that most of the people living in slums are poor. When people are poor, they cannot afford the basic necessities. Moreover, it is not possible for any government to provide these to all of its residents. Thus, people who live with poverty and cannot afford to have a shelter begin to live in a vacant place, which ultimately turns into slums. This situation can be illustrated through Fig. 4.1.

Causes of Formation of Slums in Bangladesh

One of the main features of Bangladesh is its population, which is over 160 million. The country is expected to be recognized as a developing country by 2024. Despite massive development, many people are still living under the extreme poverty line (United Nations 2008; WSUP 2007).

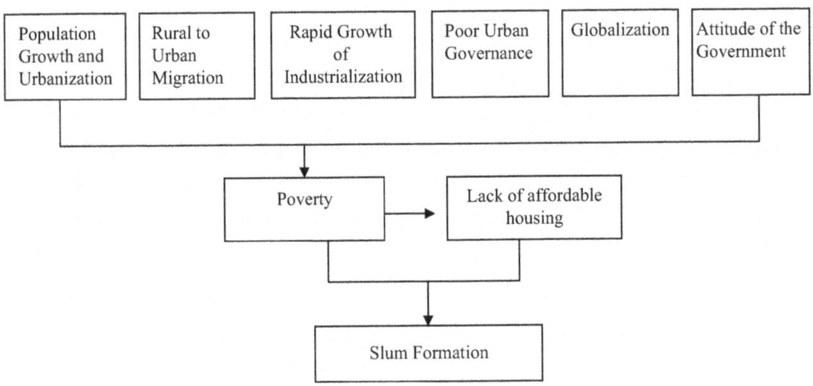

Fig. 4.1 Process of formation of slums. (Source: The figure is drawn by the author in line with the UN-Habitat, (2003))

The growth of urbanization in the country is so high that more than 40% of the people would start living in urban cities by 2030. In fact, Dhaka has turned into a megacity with a stupendous growth of population, exceeding 20 million (CUS et al. 2006). Around 300,000 to 400,000 people migrate to Dhaka city each year in search of jobs, which poses a severe challenge to the city administration as they begin living in urban slums (WSUP 2007).

The above discussion sheds light on identifying factors that contribute to the formation of urban slums globally. The subsequent section deals with identifying different factors that tend to influence slum formation, especially in the context of Bangladesh.

Hasty Growth of Urbanization

It is well known that like other Asian cities, Bangladesh has been experiencing rapid growth in urbanization.[1] Dhaka, for instance, which is the largest city in Bangladesh, has been attracting more people than any other city. However, it does not mean that the rate of urbanization in other big cities like Chittagong, Khulna, Rajshahi and others is low. Once people move into cities and get jobs, their top-most priority is to search for houses to live in. Once they find that the rate of housing is very high, they begin to reside in vacant places preferably close to their workplace. As time passes, this sort of place turns into a slum.

Another issue is that urbanization in several places across the globe is based on industrialization, while in the context of Bangladesh, it is still labor-intensive. Thus, there is a growing need for labor in the cities, which ultimately motivates rural people to move to the cities.

Diminishing Cultivable Land and Decline of Income from the Agrarian Sector

The Bangladeshi economy is still agriculture based. Thus, most of the workforce has remained engaged in the agriculture sector for its livelihood. Agricultural productivity depends to a large extent on the weather. Thus, there is a possibility that the productivity in this sector could decline

[1] The urban population in Bangladesh totals 27% (2008 estimate). And the rate of urbanization is 4.5% (2005–2010 estimate), Retrieved from http://www.eoearth.org/article/Urbanization_Rates_of_Countries, on 25/10/2010.

due to different types of natural calamities. On the other hand, population growth over the years has caused a reduction in the number of cultivable lands. However, there is a tendency among farmers to use higher fertilizer and pesticides in order to increase productivity. The combined effect of natural disasters and the shrinking amount of agricultural land along with declining productivity have affected job opportunities for day laborers negatively. In addition to these factors, the small-holding farmer does not get loans at a lower rate, and tends to become landless within a few years. By and large, these factors combined have contributed to the decline of income from the agricultural sector. As a result, people with no education or low education do not find enough job opportunities in rural areas. Thus, finding no other alternatives, people are compelled to live in urban slums, since housing in cities like Dhaka becomes a very expensive proposition.

Migration-Led Push and Pull Factors

One of the most important factors that have led to the formation of urban slums in Bangladesh is migration, especially due to environmental hazards. Moreover, Bangladesh's geographical position is predisposed to the negative effects of global warming. Consequently, the country continues to face natural calamities like *Sidr* and *Aila*. Natural disasters coupled with sustained ecological changes are therefore primary push factors for rural people of this country to migrate to urban slums.

On the other hand, the pull factors include job opportunities, better education, better health care options, and an open society. In this case, the rural populace migrates in search for betterment in all aspects. However, once they do move to the cities, the cost of living drives them to the urban slums.

Sociocultural Compulsions

In Bangladeshi society, the condition of women is not very encouraging. In rural areas, there are umpteen cases where women are left to fend for themselves. These include the destitute, divorcees and/or widows. In course of time, these women become a liability to their respective families, and become vulnerable ill-treatment. This often compels them to move to cities; while some work as day laborers, others work in construction firms, and some of them even become sex-workers. As these women do not earn enough, they are again compelled to live in urban slums.

Poor Urban Governance

Another reason that slums develop is poor urban governance. As stated before, the growth of urbanization in Bangladesh is very high. Even the government is eager to accelerate this growth. But, the rights and entitlements of the poor living in urban slums do not receive enough priority in government agendas. Having been denied incorporation into urban planning, these people start living in unhygienic conditions without proper amenities of life, which ultimately accelerates the process of expansion of urban slums. From the government's standpoint, they seem helpless, as they too do not have enough resources to cater to the needs of these migrants. In short, it is a question of a demand–supply mismatch. However, on the flip side, the government is also often criticized for their inefficiency, whereby at times, they fail to even assess the needs and demands of these migrants.

Reactions of the Government

Thus, as stated in the earlier paragraph, the government's attitude is certainly one of the primary reasons for migrants to live in urban slums. For instance, if we were to consider Dhaka, it is evident that the number of slum dwellers has risen phenomenally in the recent past. Studies suggest that within the next decade or so, the rise will be so exponential that it will be very difficult for the government to handle the situation. Nevertheless, one cannot deny the fact that this situation has not happened in a day, but over decades. The government has not paid enough attention to the rehabilitation of the people living in the slums during the initial stage. Some initiatives, albeit in a limited scale, were taken by different government agencies; but there was nothing in place to deal with the housing or land tenure security. These initiatives were rather directed for upgrading the slums. Thus, the size of the slums vis-à-vis the number of slum dwellers has multiplied over the years.

Growing Trend of Garment Industry

The garments industry in the country has been growing very fast. This sector employs thousands of workers. Importantly, as getting a job within this sector is easier, people from all corners of the country, rush to Dhaka in search of employment here.

The discussion above has been focused on identifying potential causes of urban slum formation in Bangladesh. In the following discussion, we look to explore different types of initiatives that were implemented for upgrading the situation of slum dwellers in Bangladesh.

Slum-Upgrading Initiatives in Bangladesh

Slum upgrading refers to the improvement of the existing infrastructure of the slums in the form of providing safe water, hygienic sanitation facilities, well-managed drainage systems, adequate supply of electricity, better education and health facilities, among others. Generally, construction of houses is not considered as slum upgradation, as residents could opt to do this by themselves. However, there could be government-driven programs that could offer loans for construction or improvements of houses. One of the most important components of slum upgradation includes the transfer of land tenure rights to slum dwellers at an affordable price. Herein, one needs to note that slum upgradation is an alternative to slum clearance and relocation, which in turn could possibly minimize disturbance to the social and economic life of the community people. This sort of upgradation initiatives could actually help the quality of living standards of the people living in the urban slums.

Many international organizations, donors, and community groups, and the government of Bangladesh are now addressing the increasing plight of urban slums. For making the discussion lucid and clear, we can categorize different slum-upgrading initiatives as (1) community-driven initiatives, (2) government driven initiatives, (3) donor-driven initiatives and (4) NGO-driven initiatives.

Community-Driven Initiatives

Community-driven slum upgradation is a relatively new phenomenon. Different donor agencies have been offering funds to mobilize communities for their own upgradation. It has widely been advocated that without community engagement, any slum upgradation initiative will be difficult to sustain. But, in the context of Bangladesh, it is very difficult to find cases where a community without any support from the NGOs or donor agencies has mobilized and started working for their own upgradation. However, it does not necessarily mean that such cases are absent. The following two cases deserve special mention in this regard, since these initiatives have been taken by the community people, without any support from any external forces.

Slum Welfare Cooperative Society

People living in slums in Khaiagaon area, for instance, off eastern Dhaka, formed "Provati Bastee Kalyan Samabaya Samity", or Slum Welfare Cooperative Society, putting their hands together for their own initiative. The main intention of forming this society was to address different challenges that they were confronted with. They started saving TK 1 per month in order to make a reserve, through which they could (1) improve their housing; (2) build on-site; (3) have affordable infrastructure in terms of safe drinking water, improved road facilities, hygienic sanitation, clean drains, and so on; and (4) find lands elsewhere to relocate other members of the slums. One of the salient features of this cooperative society was that despite their hardships and low income, they could manage to raise a decent capital to improve their living conditions. Earlier studies have found that the formation of the society actually helped them garner also employment opportunities, which helped in raising and/or generating household incomes. The initial days were tough, whereby they could not afford to venture into larger projects requiring substantial capital (e.g. housing and infrastructural facilities). However, over a period of time they managed to do even that. (Retrieved from http://web.mit.edu/urbanupgrading/upgrading/case-examples/ce-BG-slum-wel.html, on 26/06/2018).

Kingshuk Multipurpose Cooperative Society[2]

This project is another classic example that portrays people's capacity to solve their housing-related problems without any financial support from any other actors. The project initial comprised of seven friends who began

[2] All information about this program has been collected from http://72.167.179.155/kingshuk/history.htm, For more information about operational strategy, we will have to visit the office of Kingshuk.

saving US$1 each month in 1987. Within a span of two years (i.e. 1989), the number of people rose to 77. In commemoration of the tragic death of one of the seven friends, they organized a book fair, established a community library, implemented a neighborhood cleaning program, and organized a blood donation program. Once these six friends completed their university education in 1991, they formed a cooperative with 121 active voting members. The society expanded to 5000 project members. The society had a provision that allowed any member to withdraw their share in excess of the bank interest rate. With that saving, the society bought a low-cost land near the city to commence construction of a housing project, initially with own funds saved with the society. Additionally, 20 other members from the project team paid matching funds from their own budget. The members agreed that their saving in Kingshuk would be withdrawn slowly. The process of buying lands continued, while keeping the provision of fund withdrawal by the members from the society's account when they commenced their personal construction. Following this process, the members of the society developed a good number of buildings with their own finances (Retrieved from http://72.167.179.155/kingshuk/history.htm; on 14/11/2017).

Government-Driven Initiatives

The government of Bangladesh has relatively been less engaged in slum upgradation programs; but, there are a few notable initiatives in this regard as well. Some of the classic examples include the Local Partnerships for Urban Poverty Alleviation Project (LPUPAP), and Slum Improvement Project (SIP).

Local Partnerships for Urban Poverty Alleviation Project (LPUPAP)

Based on the recommendations of the United Nations Development Programs (UNDP) and financial assistance from the UN-Habitat, the Ministry of Local Government, Rural Development & Cooperatives initiated the LPUPAP project. This was later executed by the Local Government Engineering Division (LGED) during 2000 2007. The project objective was to develop the capacity of three cities and eight cities, respectively, to deal with the issue of poverty reduction using different mechanisms including community action planning, capacity-building, micro-finance and vocational training. During 2000–2007, the project targeted around 600,000 people who came under extreme poverty. In order to engage the poor in different types of entrepreneurial activities, the project inspired the community people to raise funds through community-based savings. They also implemented different types of training programs in line with community action planning, so that they address their most persistent needs through designing of different subprojects. Through different activities, LPUPA was found to be successful in attaining its desired objectives. The first phase was completed in 2007, whereby 11 cities were formed outside Dhaka as the main city (Retrieved from www.unchs.org; on 12/07/2017).

Although the program was designed with a high ambition of changing the situation of the urban poor, Islam et al. (2006) in their studies found that the extremely poor were kept away from the reach of the program. The second phase of the program commenced from July 2007. In the second phase, the cost of the project ($120 million) was six times higher than the cost of the first phase ($18 million). Having gained experience from the first phase, the concerned authorities brought about some modifications, while implementing the second phase. These included the incorporation of physical planning and improvement to housing along with infrastructure development. Notably, in the first phase, the main city of Dhaka was totally ignored; however, some areas of Dhaka were included in the second phase.

Urban Partnerships for Poverty Reduction Project (UPPRP)[3]

UPPRP was the extended version or the second phase of the LPUPAP that planned to incorporate the extremely poor in their target groups. Moreover, the coverage of the project was also extended to services like housing apart from infrastructure. It also aimed at carrying forward different activities implemented during the LPUPAP phase. Having started the implementation in 2007, the project intended to provide services to around 30 lakh people who lived under the extreme poverty line, comprising women and girls. One of the prime features of the project was that it

[3] All information regarding UPPR has been collected from http://webapps01.un.org/nvp/frontend!policy.action?id=192.

intended to augment the process of poverty eradication by trailing strategies that would enable poor families to build the resources, knowledge and skills through which they could increase their income and assets. UPPR also intended to contribute to the process of urban poverty reduction through providing direct employment to the urban poor in local industries and businesses, by supporting community entrepreneurs with technology transfers, targeted to improve methods of production and marketing, and by inspiring "backyard production" of urban and peri-urban food and meat (Retrieved from http://webapps01.un.org/nvp/frontend!policy.action?id=192; on 23/04/2017).

Slum Improvement Project (SIP)

Providing basic utilities to the urban poor living in slums has always been an important challenge for the government of Bangladesh. With financial assistance from UNICEF, the Local Government Engineering Department (LGED) implemented the Slum Improvement Project (SIP). This project was intended to improve the situation of slum dwellers through the development of infrastructure, improvement of primary health care, provisioning credit lines to the urban poor, while ensuring empowerment of women. As a matter of fact, the main thrust of SIP, designed in 1985 was to bring about positive changes in the lifestyle of slum people by engaging them in mobilizing resources and strengthening their access to resources owned by the government. A total of 57 slums from 5 medium towns were included for the intervention in the first phase of SIP. Starting the second phase in 1990, it extended to 185 slum clusters in 25 cities by 1994, where 40,000 women were brought under the purview (Menon n.d.). One of the notable features of SIP was that it encouraged community involvement, specifically the participation of women in the project activities. The notable advantages of SIP included (1) establishing successful women organizations under different slum communities, whereby they were assigned different social and economic roles; (2) bringing about expansions in the physical environment of slums that included construction of new footpaths and access roads, proper drainage system, building toilets, installing tube-wells, etc.; (3) increasing the family income of the slum dwellers, as a result of an effective functioning of extended credit lines and savings component of the program; and lastly, (4) increasing community awareness levels on issues related to health, sanitation and community participation (Menon n.d.: 17). Despite having some limitations, the project through its participatory approach was successful in accelerating the process of providing better basic physical, social and economic services to the urban poor.

NGO-Driven Initiatives

Different NGOs have also been working on upgrading the plight of slum dwellers across the country. However, Dhaka being the center, most of their initiatives have focused on Dhaka-based slums. But, it does not necessarily mean that the NGOs did not operate in slum-upgrading programs beyond Dhaka. The following few initiatives deserve special appreciation, since these programs have been successful in bringing about changes in the living standards of the slum dwellers.

DSK's[4] Initiative to Improve Rights to Services for Slum Dwellers in Dhaka

Previously, access to water supply was not given to households without legal entitlements to land in the cities. Like other cities, slum dwellers of Dhaka city who did not have land ownership could not have access to water from the Dhaka Water Supply and Sewerage Authority (hereinafter DWASA). Considering the misery of the slum dwellers, Dushtha Shasthya Kendra (hereinafter DSK), a Dhaka-based NGO took the initiative to help these people get legal access to water and sanitation services. Further, DSK, in partnership with WaterAid, Bangladesh began to play the role of a catalyst in setting up a connection between DWASA and the people living in slums, who wanted access to water. However, DSK found it very difficult to influence the DWASA authority to include slum dwellers in the list of its consumers. They had to spend several days and months before they could finally convince the DWASA authority.

DSK advocated providing legal water connection to the people living in slums who did not have legal land ownership. In addition, they made security deposits that guaranteed bill payments by the community members. As a result of this effort, two water-points were approved by the DWASA in underprivileged areas of Dhaka in the years 1992 and 1994, respectively.

[4] For more information regarding operational strategy of this program, we will have to visit the head office of DSK.

Being influenced by the success of two initiatives, DSK put their effort to transform this experience into a replicable model for sustainable water supply for the urban poor with an expectation that the less privileged groups of people may receive water supply from the government authorities and can be reliable customers. Finally, they were successful in influencing the DWASA to initiate a pilot project of this model in 12 slum communities in Dhaka, with a condition that all payments of the water supply would be paid following the rules of the existing institutional framework (den Bold et al. 2010).

Having received the approval from the DWASA, they started negotiating with the then Dhaka City Corporation (DCC), since they were required to build water-points on roads where ownership belonged to DCC. Finally, they were successful in obtaining permission from the DCC to set up water-points by cutting the roads that were owned by the DCC. Further, in order to ensure the channelling of funds required for the piloting a number of donor agencies, including the UNDP-World Bank Water and Sanitation Program, the Swiss Agency for Development and WaterAid Bangladesh provided kick-off loans along with all technical supports. The main intention of the pilot project was to ensure that the Water Utility Agency and potential user communities work in a coordinated manner so that changes could take place at the local institutional environment, which in turn could accelerate the process of ensuring safe water supply to the urban poor (Jinnah 2007). After 16 years of regular payments of bills, the DWASA issued a landmark decision in 2008 according to which the right was given to Community-based Organizations (CBOs) to apply for water connections on their own without the support of an intermediary. Nowadays, people living in slum communities are respected customers of the DWASA, and the scheme was implemented throughout the country (den Bold et al. 2010).

Advancing Sustainable Environmental Health (ASEH) Project[5]

The Advancing Sustainable Environmental Health (ASEH) project was started in 2005 by Nabolok with financial support from WaterAid, Bangladesh.[6] The coverage of the project was extended to 95 slums of

[5] For more detail about the operational strategy of the program, we will have to visit the office of WaterAid, Bangladesh.

[6] For details about the project, please visit http://www.nabolokbd.org/urban.htm.

ward numbers 1, 3, 21, 22, 24, 25, and 31 of Khulna City Corporation. Men, women, adolescents and children of these wards were divided into a number of community-based organizations. This was done to prepare them to stand against any sort of tyranny that could be caused by the local power structure. Additionally, these groups were also created to enable people to claim their services from the actors on the supply side. The total number of people included in the project scope was 45,062, belonging to 9403 families. Using both software and hardware approaches, Nabolok remained devoted to ensuring sustainable development in the standard of life and livelihood of these people. The project was committed to attain a number of objectives that included: (1) increase awareness about the health, hygiene and water and sanitation (WATSAN) of the people living in slums under intervention wards; (2) create opportunities for safe water and sanitation, while ensuring the people get access; (3) ensure sustainability of existing sanitation facilities, while making sure that these facilities are properly maintained; and lastly, (4) increase the participation of different stakeholders, including the local government, and CBOs so that the project is implemented successfully and effectively (Retrieved from http://www.nabolokbd.org/urban.htm: on 24/06.2018).

Disaster Management Program (DMP)

Promotion of an effective preparedness and response system in relation to national disasters was the main objective of the design of the Disaster Management Program. This project intended to meet the needs of vulnerable people, including women, children and the elderly, especially in terms of water, sanitation and food, particularly during and after natural disasters. In order to attain the objectives, a partnership among the central, the local government and NGOs was given special importance, so that a sustainable disaster preparedness system could be found out.

The fourth Integrated Food Security Program (IFSP) of the DMP component covered 1970 unions in 265 Upazilas in 58 districts of Bangladesh. As regards the scope of the intervention, the fourth phase was completely different, as it covered most of the districts of the country. Upazilas were chosen based on incidents of natural disasters and calamities. Thus, most of the country was exposed to the intervention of the component. Like the Upazilas, the unions were also chosen based on the result of risk analysis that was carried out by the DMP team in 1995 in association with the CARE Monitoring and Evaluation team. The project attained a great deal of success by ensuring food security of vulnerable people under the project intervention areas (CARE, Bangladesh 2002a).

Population Services and Training Centre's (PSTC) Support in Chanpara Slum during the Pilot Phase[7]

Located 6 km away from the capital, Dhaka, Chon Para Bashtohara Punorbashon Kendro (which is known as Chanpara slum) is one of the largest slums, covering an area of 1 km. It was first established by the government of Bangladesh in 1975 for rehabilitating landless people of Dhaka city. At the elementary phase, around 5000 families were shifted there. However, in due course of time, the population has been on the rise. By 2006, around 38,000 people of 7766 families started living there (Ahmed 2006). Other than electricity and a few concrete roads, most of the people of this slum were deprived of modern amenities of urban life. Considering the maladies of these people, water supply and sanitation programs began to be implemented in Chanpara slum by the Population Services and Training Centre (PSTC) in 2000; 10% population of this slum came under this program through the installation of 38 tube wells and 114 pit latrines by the end of 2003. During that time 100% capital cost for toilets and tube wells were recovered, apart from the office and management costs. One of the interesting findings of this program was that it excluded the most vulnerable groups from the category of service recipients (Ahmed 2006).

Slum Development by SHEVA—Centre for Women and Children's Welfare[8]

Through the implementation of this project, SHEVA has established the fact that interventions from NGOs could indeed improve the living standards of the slum dwellers through their role as intermediaries that motivate the owners and occupiers to work jointly. SHEVA started working with 40 beneficiary families that were dependent on informal sector jobs with an average income of about US$50–70/month. The living condition

[7] For more detail about the operational strategy of the program, we will have to visit the office of PSTC.

[8] All information about this program has been collected from http://www.shevabd.org/ongoing_programs.htm, for more information about this program we will have to visit head office of SHEVA.

of these families was miserable, as they were compelled to stay in impermanent structures at the cost of US$8 for 6–8 m^2 rooms in six *bastees* (600 m^2). Taking a loan from the Basic Bank, SHEVA started implementing a "Shelter Improvement Project" on one plot, where they built semi-permanent row houses. The plan of the construction was well designed with all the amenities that urban people generally have. For instance, the building had proper ventilation, separate bathrooms and toilets, gas line in common kitchen areas, training and community meeting room, along with a covered sitting area (Retrieved from http://www.shevabd.org/ongoing_programs.htm; on 23/06/2017).

The owner of the land and SHEVA signed a rental agreement for five years. Moreover, the agreement was also signed with the tenants who expressed interest to get training on different aspects of community-based programs in the form of water and sanitation management, health care, functional education and skill development. They also agreed to pay an increased rent while expressing their commitment to abide by the community's decision in related matters. The project cost (US$20,000) was paid back at an interest rate of 12.5%.

The project cost of US$20,000 was amortized in 7.5 years at 12.5% interest. In lieu of the multiple benefits in terms of improvements, the tenants contracted to pay double as rent. Encouraged by the outcome of the project, and seeing the improvement in the living condition of the slum people, many neighborhoods expressed their interest to be involved in a similar project (Retrieved from http://www.shevabd.org/ongoing_programs.htm; on 23/06/2017).

Coalition for the Urban Poor (CUP)

Formed in 1989, Coalition for the Urban Poor (CUP) has been working as a network of NGOs who work with the urban poor. The main task of the network has been to figure out different problems and needs of the poor in urban areas, and execute proper programs to ensure that there is no duplication of efforts. CUP used an informal platform known as Bangladesh Urban Round Table (BURT). CUP contacted different donor organizations, governmental bodies, along with research and educational institutions (BURT 2005). However, CUP's coverage has remained restricted to Dhaka and Chittagong, along with a chapter in Khulna.

CUP played an important role in advocating for the preparation of the poor people-friendly national policy. CUP also tried to ensure coordination among the government and donors on the issue of policy and practice for the urban poor. It also put its efforts to negotiate with the government for preventing evictions. For instance, CUP played an important role in lobbying with the interim government on its decision to restrict evictions and to resettle eviction victims (Prothom Alo 18/03/ 2007).[9]

CUP also worked hard to guarantee the voting rights of slum residents in 1994. Their advocacy led to the formation of *the Bastee Basheer Odhikar Surakha Committees* (BOSC) (Slum-dwellers Rights Protection Committee) in 2000. The main intention of the formation of the organization was to find strategies to bring the slum residents into the social mainstream and the city governance. The findings of a study conducted by Banks (2006) suggested that the formation of (BOSCs) has empowered the slum dwellers of the city to raise their voices, and place their demands to the elected representatives of municipalities. This way, they managed to obtain access to different services, including water supply, sanitation and electricity. BOSCs worked as an intermediary for communicating with the central government policy-makers through local elected representatives of the municipalities (Banks 2006).

CARE, Bangladesh

Located in Dhaka, CARE has been working tirelessly in different parts of the world as a multinational NGO. CARE implemented an urban development initiative entitled 'Shouhardo' in 16 municipalities within a span of 5 years. The main intention of the project was to alleviate poverty of the urban poor. Having linkage with CIP-VURT, CARE-BD also implemented an "Environmental Sanitation, Hygiene and Water Supply in Urban Slums and Fringes Project". With financial assistance from UNICEF and the government of Bangladesh, the project intended to improve the sanitation and water supply of about 1 million residents of urban slums. In addition to these projects, CARE-BD also worked with the informal settlement with an intention to secure their land rights and reallocation (Hussain 2007).

[9] The interim government took the decision on 17 March 2007.

Dushtha Shaystha Kendra (DSK)

Started in 1988, DSK's main focus has remained on the delivery of primary health care services in some slums within Dhaka. Over a period of time, DSK extended their activities in different cities, including Chittagong and Khulna, along with several rural locations. Among different programs that they conducted, the water and sanitation program deserves a special mention, as it was able to convince DWASA to provide water connection to a number of informal settlements within Dhaka with no proper land rights. In this process, DSK worked as a collateral. In addition to providing access to water supply, DSK also provided support in building toilets in different slums within their purview. They also implemented programs to build awareness among slum dwellers on different issues relating to health and hygiene. One of the notable features of DSK is that they used a groundbreaking approach to work on the water and sanitation project, having close relations with all the government departments. DSK had established a network with different national and international organizations working for the betterment of the people residing in informal settlements (retrieved from http://www.dskbangladesh.org/wash-projects/; on 23/03/2017).

LOSAUK (An Organization of People's Action for Sociocultural and Economic Development)

LOSAUK is a Khulna-based social welfare research institute that began work in 1987. This organization does not provide any services to the urban poor; instead they conduct research, build awareness among the slum dwellers and carry out advocacy programs for providing better services. In fact, the organization works as a facilitator, whose main intention is to ensure social transformation. Using different cultural and theatre tools, the organization has been trying to build awareness among slum dwellers, and also form network groups with adolescent women to carry out programs for ensuring their rights, including land rights, water supply and sanitation. (http://www.losauk.org/details/index.html; accessed on 23/03/2017).

Donor-Driven Initiatives

Like other countries of the world, different donor agencies have been providing funds to the government and several NGOs for carrying out diverse slum upgradation programs for the people residing in urban slums in Bangladesh. Different programs have already been proved to be successful. The following donor-driven programs deserve special mention here.

The Integrated Food Security Program (IFSP)

The Integrated Food Security Program (IFSP) started its operations in 2000, as a Title II food security project. Supporting Household Activities for Hygiene, Assets and Revenue (SHAHAR), Building Union Infrastructure for Urban Governments (BUILD), Flood-proofing (FPP); and Disaster Management (DMP) were the four components of the IFSP. With the help of around 600 staff, the IFSP implemented its interventions in many districts. The programs were intended to attain the goal of promoting and protecting food and livelihood security of susceptible groups in both rural and urban areas (CARE, Bangladesh 2002b).

The Supporting Household Activities for Hygiene, Assets and Revenue (SHAHAR)

With the intent to ensure food security of the urban poor, the SHAHAR project (Supporting Household Activities for Hygiene, Assets and Revenue)[10] started its operations through CARE, Bangladesh in July 1999. The first pilot project began in the low-income communities of Tongi and Jessore. The main focus of SHAHAR was the urban poor and vulnerable community who were living in slums and low-income settlements in Bangladesh. Nabolok, for instance, implemented a project in Tongi Pourashava in Gazipur district. Covering four urban areas, SHAHAR implemented different components of the project for 35,000 households. Different components included four key areas. These were: urban infrastructure (including drains, footpaths, earth filling and community latrines); health, hygiene and nutrition education; community mobiliza-

[10] For more details about the SHAHAR project, please visit http://www.ifpri.org/dataset/bangladesh-2.

tion and institutional strengthening; and, income generation (Retrieved from http://www.ifpri.org/publication/jessore-and-tongi, accessed on 24/07/2017).

Building Union Infrastructure for Local Government (BUILD)

BUILD was again a part of IFSP. The project worked for the improvement of around 1250 km of R1 roads in 34 districts of the country with an intention of ensuring connectivity through these roads to different population centers and markets. Combined with the construction of roads, BUILD also launched a program for tree plantation, which was to ensure stabilization and protection of slops, while reducing the possibility of erosions. Under this program, 800,000 trees were planted by 1000 destitute women along 550 km of roads. Those women who remained engaged in tree plantation were paid a monthly salary that extended up to 26 months. They were also given the ownership of selling the tree when it was in full bloom (CARE, Bangladesh 2002b).

As part of the second component, BUILD carried out different capacity development programs of the elected representatives of the local government bodies with the expectation that they would discharge their responsibilities as part of their civic responsibilities. This would strengthen democratic practices, and help in decentralizing the decision–making process. Through various trainings, the project intended to increase the managerial and leadership skills of the elected local government officials along with the UP secretaries. In order to ensure transparency and accountability of the local government bodies, an arrangement was made for holding a meeting with stakeholder groups and UP representatives. Through these activities, the project tried to augment the process of participation of marginalized and vulnerable groups including women. This involved the process of planning and decision-making both of the local government bodies and other stakeholders. Additionally, this also brought forth the gender dimension of local government activities. The ultimate objectives of the project were to make sure that the local government officials would play a proactive role in creating opportunities for the participation of the community in the local government planning and decision-making (CARE, Bangladesh 2002b).

Secondary Towns Water Supply and Sanitation Sector Project (STWSSSP)

The Community-Driven Development (CDD) approach was used by the Asian Development Bank (ADB) in most of their interventions in the field of water supply and sanitation services in Bangladesh. Around half of the projects financed by ADP during 2001–2007 used CDD as one of the striking features, while working in the water supply and sanitation departments. ADB started the implementation of a US$7.1 million project entitled "Small Towns Water Supply and Sanitation Sector Project (STWSSSP)[11]" in 2006, where ADB's contribution was US$42 million (ADB 2009). In order to ensure maximum reachability of water supply and sanitation services to 16 secondary towns (Purashavas), it demanded a performance-driven approach from all its stakeholders. One of the main features of the project was that it advocated for involving NGOs and CBOs in the service delivery process, especially in the field of water and sanitation. The objective behind this move was to contribute to the improvement of service delivery in such situations where the centralized service delivery has failed to respond to the needs and demands of the service receivers (ADB 2009).

Conclusion

The speedy growth of urbanization in different parts of the world has been facilitating expansion and complexity in cities, while posing new challenges for the urban poor in living a decent life. South Asia, in general, and Bangladesh, in particular, is not an exception in this regard. The enormous growth of the urban population has been creating serious problems, especially with regard to urban housing, due to which a large part of the population is compelled to live in slums. Along with the growing number of population, other factors like rapid rural–urban migration, poor urban governance, the rapid growth of industrialization, globalization, and attitude of the government have been facilitating the process of the formation of slums in cities. In order to overcome the situation that is caused due to expansion of slum population, different initiatives have been taken by both government and nongovernmental organizations. Some of the

[11] More information about the project can be found at: https://www.adb.org/projects/documents/lao-stwsssp-feb-2016-iee.

programs have become successful, while others have failed to produce the desired level of success. The next chapter sheds light on the global best practices of urban slum development initiatives.

References

Ahmed, R. (2006, November). *A case study on reaching the poorest & vulnerable*. A paper presented in 32nd WEDC conference, Colombo, Sri Lanka. Retrieved May 23, 2010, from http://www.wateraid.org/documents/plugin_documents/case_study__reaching_the_poorest_and_most_vulnerable__pstc.pdf.

Asian Development Bank. (2009). *Community-driven development country profile*. Bangladesh. Retrieved June 10, 2010, from http://www.adb.org/Documents/Participation/Country-Brief-Bangladesh.pdf.

Asian Development Bank. (2014). *Sustainable urbanization in Asia and Latin America*. Manila: Asian Development Bank and Inter-American Development Bank.

Banks, N. (2006). *A tale of two wards: Political participation and the urban poor in Dhaka City*. Working paper, Center for Governance Studies, BRAC University, Dhaka.

BURT. (2005). *Dialogue with donors on urban poverty issues*. Dhaka: CARE.

Camilo, A. C. A. (2008). *Learning from slum upgrading and participation: A case study of participatory slum upgrading in the emergence of new governance in the city of Medellín–Colombia*. KTH, Department of Urban Planning and Environment Division of Environmental Strategies Research.

CARE, Bangladesh. (2002a). *Integrated food security program (IFSP)*. Midterm Evaluation Report, Prepared by TANGO International, Inc. in collaboration with Human Development Research Centre, HDRC, Dhaka.

CARE, Bangladesh. (2002b). *Midterm evaluation of integrated food security program-IFSP*. Prepared by TANGO International, Inc in collaboration with Human Development Research centre, HDRC, Dhaka.

CUS et al. (2006). *Slums of urban Bangladesh: Mapping and census*, 2005. Dhaka: CUS (Center for Urban Studies).

den Bold, M. V., Uwejamomere, T., & Vandermeer, K. (2010). *Raising visibility and voices of the urban poor: Civil society's engagement in urban water and sanitation reform—Experiences from WaterAid country programmes*. A Report Prepared for WaterAid. Retrieved from BURT (2005) Position Paper, CARE-Bangladesh, Dhaka.

Ellis, P., & Roberts, M. (2016). *Leveraging urbanization in South Asia: Managing spatial transformation for prosperity and liveability*. Washington, DC: World Bank Group.

Hussain, D. J. (2007). *Environmental sanitation, hygiene and water supply in urban slums and fringes project (GoB-Unicef)*. Project Completion Report, Dhaka.

Islam, N., Mahbub, A., Nazem, N., Angeles, G., & Lance, P. (2006). *Slums of urban Bangladesh: Mappying and census*, 2005. Dhaka: Centre for Urban Studies, Measure Evaluation and National Institute of Population Research and Training.

Jinnah, S. I. A. (2007). *Rights of water connections for urban slum dwellers in Bangladesh: A study on DSK's experience in three slums of Mirpur*, Dhaka: WaterAid, Bangladesh. Retrieved June 2, 2010, from http://www.wateraid.org/documents/plugin_documents/water_points_for_urban_slum_dwellers.pdf.

Menon, B. (n.d.). *Informal settlement upgrading in Dhaka: Sector study. Urban housing and informal settlements in Bangladesh*. Washington, DC: World Bank.

Prothom Alo. (2007, March 18). A widely circulated national daily published from Dhaka.

Retrieved April 23, 2017, from http://webapps01.un.org/nvp/frontend!policy.action?id=192.

Retrieved August 24, 2017, from https://www.adb.org/projects/documents/lao-stwsssp-feb-2016-iee.

Retrieved from June 23, 2017, from http://www.shevabd.org/ongoing_programs.htm.

Retrieved July 12, 2017, from www.unchs.org.

Retrieved July 24, 2017, from http://www.ifpri.org/publication/jessore-and-tongi.

Retrieved July 25, 2017, from http://www.ifpri.org/dataset/bangladesh-2.

Retrieved June 24, 2018, from http://www.nabolokbd.org/urban.htm.

Retrieved June 26, 2018, from http://web.mit.edu/urbanupgrading/upgrading/case-examples/ce-BG-slum-wel.html.

Retrieved March, 23, 2017, from http://www.dskbangladesh.org/wash-projects/.

Retrieved March 23, 2017, from http://www.losauk.org/details/index.html.

Retrieved November 12, 2018, from https://en.wikipedia.org/wiki/Cyclone_Aila.

Retrieved November 14, 2017, from http://72.167.179.155/kingshuk/history.htm.

Retrieved Number 12, 2018, from https://en.wikipedia.org/wiki/Cyclone_Sidr.

Retrieved October 25, 2010, from http://www.eoearth.org/article/Urbanization_Rates_of_Countries.

UN-DESA. (2006). *The millennium development goals report*. United Nations Department of Economic and Social Affairs, UNDP.

UN-HABITAT. (2003). *The challenge of slums: Global report on human settlements.* London and Sterling: UN-HABITAT—Earthscan Publications Ltd.

UN-HABITAT. (2007). Twenty first session of the governing council. Retrieved September 30, 2015, from http://www.unhabitat.org/downloads/docs/4625_51419_GC%2021%20What%20are%20slums.pdf.

United Nations. (2008). *World urbanization prospects: The 2007 revision database.* New York: United Nations.

United Nations. (2014). *World urbanization prospects: The 2014 revision.* Population Division, Department of Economic and Social Affairs. New York: United Nations.

Ward, D. (1976). The Victorian slum: An enduring myth? *Annals of the Association of American Geographers, 66*(2), 323–336.

WSUP. (2007). *Water and sanitation for the urban poor.* Scoping report. Water and Sanitation for the Urban Poor (WSUP), London.

CHAPTER 5

Global Best Practices of Urban Slum Development

Introduction

The "slum" as a concept is not new in development literature. The concept has been used by different scholars and development practitioners for decades. Slum development has a historical past in almost every city. The issue of slum development has been gaining the attention of third-world academicians and development experts since the beginning of industrialization and urbanization in the developing world in the 1960s and 1970s.

The concentration of economic growth in the cities and the movement of people from rural to urban areas was a product of industrialization. The same thing happened in Europe and America during the Industrial Revolution, in the 1700s and 1800s.The development of slums in cities has a close relationship with rural–urban migration. Poor villagers come to view cities as a mecca where industrialization makes everyone rich by magic. So, they go there; but the villagers lack the skills and capital that made city dwellers rich. They are in the cities but they are still poor: in fact, the higher cost of living in the cities and the absence of land and housing that they had in the village makes them even poorer. They crowd into any land and housing they can find, with or without permission of the owner, lacking the income to pay rent for proper homes with amenities like water, sanitation and electricity supply. These are, by definition, slums.

Again, the same phenomenon was observed during the Industrial Revolution in Europe and America: London and New York City, in the 1800s, were disgusting places of dirt, grime, hunger, crime, child labor,

P. K. Panday, *The Face of Urbanization and Urban Poverty in Bangladesh*, https://doi.org/10.1007/978-981-15-3332-7_5

smoke, unemployment, overcrowding, dangerous homes and workplaces, fires and, yes, all of these were concentrated in slums. In America, the problem was both exacerbated by immigration and later ameliorated by frontier settlement opportunities. In Britain, the urban half of the country remained poor, its cities little more than slums, until World War II leveled the slums and full employment with a Welfare State ended poverty in the 1940s. Developing countries are not so lucky today: they have no frontiers, war does not level their slums and they cannot create Welfare States because there is no wealth to distribute. Instead of good luck, the developing countries have additional problems that Britain and America were already resolving when the Industrial Revolution occurred. Britain and America mostly ended their rather-corrupt systems of governance, especially at the local level, in the first 20 years of the twentieth century. Industrialization made much more progress, more quickly, in Britain and America in the 1800s and 1900s than it has in the developing countries since the 1960s: providing plentiful jobs with living wages to slum dwellers, which allowed them to integrate into better parts of the cities. Successful industrialization, with cleaner government, generated tax revenue that allowed the introduction of social security benefits, free and compulsory education, housing regulation and free or subsidized health care, initially for the poor by targeted welfare payments, which provided slum dwellers a basic minimum standard of living in Britain and America and allowed them to work and study their way out of poverty. America and Britain subsidized agricultural prices or set up marketing cooperatives in the 1930s, greatly slowing down the rural–urban migration problem by making farming a profitable occupation. In sharp contrast, developing countries have serious unresolved problems of corruption, rural poverty, unemployment, underemployment, low wages, shortage of tax revenue and little money for health, education and social services or enforcement of regulations, each of which perpetuates and enhances the growth of slums. Therefore, the *pull* factors of rural–urban income disparity, concentration of economic growth in cities, quality health and education facilities in the cities and a Western lifestyle in the urban areas and the *push* factors of rural poverty, poor health and education services in rural areas and low agricultural prices became irresistible to villagers—who soon became slum dwellers.

Most of the housing in the slums of developing countries is illegal. In many cases, the poor put up shacks on other people's land without seeking permission: the Turkish word for this phenomenon in Istanbul, "*gecekondu*", meaning "built overnight", says it all. These shacks are not only illegal but dangerous in storms and floods and fires waiting to start anytime. In other cases, poor tenants rent from "slumlords", as the landlords of these houses are called in America, at high rents, and who invest nothing in the buildings, which do not conform to legal requirements for safety, light, air, space, etc. Yet, in most developing countries, land title is the basis of legal entitlements to amenities like water, sewerage and power. Slum dwellers have no land title so they get none of the above.

The perceived solution to the proliferation of slums in the developing world in the late twentieth century, which was illegal anyway, was to knock them down. The United Nations (Werlin 1999) found that the Governments of developing countries destroyed more houses in the 1970s than they built. Their main effect was to create urban homelessness and a large class of transients and street dwellers. In addition, the developing nations had no resources to rehouse the huge number of rural migrants flooding into the cities from their village homes. The rate of urbanization was so fast that half the world's total population became urbanized by the late twentieth century. But one-third of these populations were suffering from inadequate access to safe drinking water, while 60% suffered from lack of access to appropriate sanitation (Sivaramakrishnan 1994). The World Bank, Governments and experts realized by the end of the twentieth century that "slum clearance", knocking down buildings in the slums, was not solving the problem of slums and creating new problems of its own.

Therefore, in the twenty-first century, the consensus of experts, non-government organizations, Governments and others is not "slum clearance" but rather "slum upgrading". Upgrading means trying to find ways to improve the standard of living for slum dwellers rather than driving them out of the slums. Every citizen of a country has the legitimate right to live with dignity and basic amenities that meet their physical needs. If the city government does not do something for slum dwellers, not just for landlords who want squatters off their land, they face unrest, crime, perpetuation of the slums and a permanently unstable condition in the slums. Also many political parties have come to realize that slum dwellers may not have much but they do have votes to give Governments that help them. So this book concentrates on slum upgrading and what works. The book gives a critical analysis of some of the noteworthy slum development initiatives that have attained success. These success stories are most commonly known as "best practices".

What Is a "Best Practice"?

Generally, best practice means success stories. When it concerns the best practices of urban slum development initiatives, it refers to those projects that have attained a high degree of success in meeting their goals as a result of their implementation. These success stories could be used as examples for other projects. However, there is hardly any uniform definition or characteristics of best practices, as various scholars have used different criteria to conduct the benchmarking of best practices (Keehley et al. 1997).

If any project is to be a best practice, it must prove itself successful for several years. The success of these programs must have been highlighted by scholars and practitioners as useful approaches if we want to present them as models to other projects or organizations that lack success. To be a best practice, the project must be able to portray a clear vision with a contrast, showing insight, with the accepted truth. The practice of the project must show originality and novelty, and stand the test of scholarship about its practice. The project should be radical, producing striking, positive benefits, not merely incremental steps forward (Senge 1990). The project, while effective as it is, must be "stretchy", meaning able to be adjusted to different conditions, not merely a product of its environment that cannot work elsewhere. These features will make these practices replicable in different contexts with required modifications (Hiebeler et al. 1998: 21). On the other hand, Keehley et al. (1997: 27) have argued that, in order to be replicable and successful, a best practice must produce quantifiable results in the form of output, outcome, timeliness, efficiency or effectiveness. To be a best practice, the project must not just be "striking" to us, who read about it: it must leave its target beneficiaries feeling "struck" by something excellent in their lives.

Some other features of best practices include customer–friendliness, in order to be acceptable to a large number of clients and the project must ensure a congenial working environment, with good interaction between the clients and the staff of an organization. In cases where quantifying the result is not possible, a best practice can be accessible by of the context in which the exercise has contributed to the attainment of its goals, missions and objectives. Based on the above discussion, we can conclude that, above all, a best practice is something that is sustainable because everyone, both within the organization and outside, interacting with it or studying it, knows that it works.

Beyond that inner sense of "Yes, this works", objective criteria are needed to be sure that the best practices really are best. "Best" implies comparison with other projects that do not reach that standard and gut feelings do not let us make those kinds of judgments in an intelligible or defensible way: criteria do. The best criteria would, ideally, come from the target group of the project, as they know best what they need and whether the project has really helped them to get what they need or not.

Yet there is a lot that the target group does not know: the success of an intervention, in practice, rests greatly on the efficiency of the administrators, the support of the financing agencies, the ideologies behind the origin of the interventions and the positive role of different actors who are interested in the outcome of the intervention (Øyen 2004). Ultimately, the success of the intervention depends on those who "own" it. There are few projects in the real world that become successful merely by satisfying their users, without administrative expertise and serious finance.

So the best form of intervention allows the users to raise their voices to get what they need to professional administrators, who really do listen and try their best to satisfy them through the work of the project. In such cases, the users can exercise their right to define the criteria of adjudicating "best practice" by voicing their expectations from the intervention, because the project co-opts those expectations as its own expectations of itself. This should be the ideal type of model for identifying the best practice.

One criticism of this model is that there might be many users with inadequate knowledge of the context in which they, and the project, function. Thus, their demands may be either unrealistic or, having been granted, not really improve their situation. Then, the target group can blame the project and say it is not good practice because it did not meet their needs.

So, defining one "best" practice *only* within the criteria of best practice as perceived by the target groups would not be realistic. In this book, I have referred to those programs as best practices that have attained success not only in the view of their target groups but by withstanding the test of time, in the view of objective scholars and others who evaluate them, and by inspiring other projects in their country and other countries to follow their examples.

For example, on the important issue of urban poverty reduction, which all of the best slum-upgrading projects must act upon, we do not insist that the project, by itself, has eliminated poverty in the slum or even reduced it significantly, although, without doubt, this will be the criterion on which the poor will judge it. Rather, it is sufficient that the program has continued to make significant progress in reducing poverty over time and has at least ensured that the poor are not worse off and that their numbers have not been significantly augmented, for an urban poverty project to be a best practice. Furthermore, a project is more likely to be a best practice if it makes progress against many different types of urban poverty, not just having effect in a limited area or against a single cause of urban poverty (Øyen 2004).

Calcutta' s Basti Improvement Program (BIP)

In response to the concerns of the World Health Organization (WHO) about the state of public health in Calcutta in the early 1960s, the Ford Foundation provided financial assistance to prepare and develop a Basic Development Plan for the city in the period 1966–1986. During that time, another megaproject, called the "Calcutta Urban Development Program (CUDP)", in the 1970s, was financed by the World Bank.

The Basti Improvement Program (BIP) was one of the major components of the CUDP. The major objectives of the BIP were: (i) the transformation of all unsanitary latrines into sanitary latrines; (ii) provide water taps and improvement of the drainage services; (iii) building and extension of roads and pathways; (iv) establishment of road lighting; and (v) ensure effective disposal facilities for waste within the *basties (Slums)*.[1]

The implementation of the BIP was a success story as it brought positive change of nearly 67% of the slums of Calcutta, with a population of 3 million people (Pugh 1990). The implementation of the project reduced the death rate from waterborne diseases in Calcutta, including cholera (Werlin 1999), during the 1970s, by nearly 50%.

Unfortunately, the progress made by the project during its life did not continue after it was phased out in 1986. The population of the slums continued to rise, until presently 300–400 people are using a toilet that was set up for only 25 people. The BIP also was unable to make significant progress against the housing problem in Kolkata. The main hindrances for

[1] In 1977 when the Left Front Government came into power in the State of West Bengal, the State Government nationalized most of the *basti* lands. However, the courts stopped the Government from carrying out any development of this land by deciding that the intermediary tenants have the first right to develop the *basti*. The Government later enacted legislation restricting the rights of the intermediate tenants, but the court decision still protected the security of the tenant dwellers.

BIP were the unwillingness of the beneficiaries to pay for the services they received and the inability or unwillingness of the Government of West Bengal to address the problem of the ever-increasing squatter settlements in and around Kolkata (Thomas 1997). In the end, the urban government bodies that remain responsible for the maintenance of the infrastructure, drainage and sanitation created problems during the implementation of the project, which, therefore, could not proceed further.

Comprehensive Kampung Improvement Program (KIP) in Surabaya, Indonesia

Kampung refers to the informal and self-planned (unplanned) settlements in Indonesian cities. Kampung constitutes a large share of urban settlements in Indonesia. In Indonesia, Kampungs are not treated as "slums". Instead, these were considered as ill-managed and poor housing that needed sewerage systems, collection of garbage and other municipal facilities. During the late 1960s, the national government of Indonesia used to bear the responsibilities of improving the living condition in these Kampungs. It was done in order to engage community people in the process of the delivery of services and make improvements in physical infrastructure. Under the auspices of the Government, the process started in Jakarta and Surabaya in 1968. Although Kampungs only covered 7% of the city areas in the 1960s, around 63% of the Surabaya population started living in these Kampungs in 1993. Despite the low budget of the national government for Kampung improvement, the projects became a success story within a few years, due to the extensive support and engagement of the community people in this process. In 1975, when the World Bank confirmed that they would provide assistance for the implementation of the KIP, the Government extended the scope of KIP service by including health and environmental aspects along with basic infrastructure. KIP served more than 60% of the population of the cities despite the fact that only one-fifth of the city budget was spent through KIP. One of the notable features of the program was that the majority of the low-income group people were brought under the services. In recognition of its success, the Surabaya won different international prizes, including the Aga Khan Award for Architecture (1986), UNEP Award (1990), and the Habitat Award (1991) (Dhakal 2002). From 1984 to 1990, KIP attained the following landmarks:

- The living condition of 1.2 million people was improved
- 220 km of footpaths and roads were elevated
- 93 km of new drains and culverts were built
- 56,000 meters of water pipes were placed
- 86 public bathing, washing, and toilet facilities were constructed
- The solid waste collection was improved to a great extent
- A number of primary schools and centers of public health were constructed

After gaining initial success, the city of Surabaya invested more effort in extending the coverage of the program during the mid-1990s. Along with other sectors, their focus was concentrated on nonphysical aspects, in the form of bringing changes in the socioeconomic condition of the inhabitants in Kampungs or the development of the community. The need for the new dimension was considered to be serious as a wide gap in terms of development was observed among the Kampungs and the rest of the cities. That is why more efforts were made on improving the socioeconomic conditions of the people within Kampungs. Consequently, the extended and revised version of the project, titled the Comprehensive Kampung Improvement program (CKIP), was implemented during 1998–2002 in 27 Kampungs (Dhakal 2002). The main objectives of C-KIP were to:

- Intensify the level of awareness of the community people about different problems and potentials of Kampungs
- Inspire the community to start to identify their needs and obstacles and also find ways to solve those
- Mobilize the community to get involved in the process of their own planning, implementation and evaluation
- Make the community capable of mobilizing resources for the projected increase in the capacity of the community to face different challenges associated with the social-economic aspect of their life

C-KIP Community Participation Model

As stated earlier, the basis of C-KIP was the success story of KIP. Influenced by the success of KIP, it was replicated in other cities of Indonesia and in some other cities of Vietnam, Cambodia, Thailand, India, etc. One of the notable features of C-KIP was that it stressed the importance of the engagement of the community in the process of planning, implementation and evaluation of development plans, along with the local government and other supporting organizations. Accordingly, communities got involved in the process of making decisions for their own development on the basis of their needs and priorities. Most importantly, a sense of ownership was developed among the community people about the C-KIP that helped them to remain involved in all developmental projects. The basis of all of their programs was an estimate of their own resources as well as their demands. One significant advantage of this type of project was that this could motivate the residents of the city to own such initiatives and put their best efforts to implement all the programs within the stipulated budget or mobilize funds from their own sources to assist the city authority. A C-KIP project began implementation following a multistage development process (Ostrom et al. 1993).

Community Self-Survey

Conducting a survey of its residents was the initial phase of the project execution. The main task of the survey was to figure out the problems and opportunities within the community. In the survey, mapping was done using quantitative methods. Accordingly, planning was done taking into consideration the mapping. Ensuring the active engagement of the community members in the survey, all the problems and opportunities of the community were identified for incorporation in the plans. While mapping, five issues including: (i) situation of housing, (ii) availability and quality of services, (iii) availability and worth of infrastructures, (iv) position of the community and (v) reinforced features (group, involvement, etc.) were considered. For instance, while taking decision on the physical infrastructure, different aspects like pathway development, management of solid waste, improvement of water supply, public toilets and so on were considered. In the category of nonphysical-infrastructure-related decisions, issues like development of cooperatives, micro-credit, skill development planning and so on, were considered (Ostrom et al. 1993). Once all the problems and potentials were identified through the survey, a workshop was organized, with the presence of the community people, specialists, officials of the city government, with an intention to make a decision on what to include and what to incorporate.

Community Organizations

Once the mapping was done, the next step was to form community organizations for taking care of issues relating to the management of funds, the implementation of the programs and general management. Four kinds of community establishments were formed in C-KIP to carry out four different types of activities, including the making of decisions, management of finance, execution and oversight.

- *Making of Decisions*: All responsibilities relating to the overall management were vested in the local Kampung Development Board (KDB) (or sometimes called Kampung Foundation). One of the main responsibilities of KDB was to ensure coordination between communities who planned program and city government or bank who provided funds. Activities like dissemination of technology and information as well as the mobilizing public were also undertaken by KDB. Following bottom-up principles, members of the board were elected by local community members.
- *Finance Management Task Force*: A self-financing local cooperative mechanism entitled Multi Economic-based Cooperation (MEC) remained responsible for the management of funds and the provision of micro-credit to the community group members. One of the notable features of the micro-credit program was that it was the responsibility of the community group to pay the micro-credit rather than the individual members. Through this process, the community group could choose their members from trusted people that could help them to overcome the problem of 'free riding" by some individuals. "Free riders" were scrutinized by a local organization. There was a provision for examining the capacity of the members to repay the micro-credit by the representatives of the MEC, who did so by interviews. Once the examination was done, the representative could recommend someone for the loan or training before the loan is disbursed (Ostrom et al. 1993; Dhakal 2002).
- *The Implementation Task Force*: The activities relating to the implementation of the program were undertaken by the Community Self-help Group (CSG) consisting of five to ten households. One of the notable features of this group was that it was comprised of people

having similar interests and needs. The group was headed by a leader who selected trusted members so that they could work with him or her effectively. The group would help him or her in setting programs and priorities and ensure compliance with the program schedule and carry out different activities. Supervision Council (SC): All activities relating to monitoring and supervision of KDB were undertaken by the supervision Council (SC). All these institutions required training for better management and the smooth progression of different activities. The need for training in these institutions was met through organizing different lectures, experts' visits and exposure visits in other successful Kampungs for information gathering. One of the significant features of C-KIP was its focus on community mobilization for identifying and solving their problems.

Formulation of Development Planning

The community self-survey was the main basis of all the development plans. While developing plans, the availability of funds was taken into consideration. When government funding was inadequate, community people mobilized resources and provided their physical resources. Moreover, all plans were developed in line with the city development plan.

Financial Mechanism

The project that was funded by the World Bank in Surabaya ended in the mid-1990s. After the completion of the World Bank project, the C-KIP started implementation for the period of 1998–2002 with funds provided by the city government from the annual maintenance budget. The direct channelling of the funds by the city government to the local communities through KDB reduced overhead costs by 30%. The Kampung was getting around 200 million Indonesian Rupiah until 2001, which rose to 250 million from 2002; 20% of the fund was dedicated as a grant for building new physical infrastructure sector, in addition to the contributions of the community's people. The rest was allocated to designing cooperative mechanisms. A standard interest rate of 12% was fixed for micro-credit, giving autonomy to each Kampung to decide the rate of interest of their own micro-credit funds (Dhakal 2002).

Role of Government and Other Stakeholders

C-KIP was initiated by the Surabaya City government, which launched C-KIP in association with its shareholders and the ITS (Institute of Technology Surabaya). Technical and other relevant support was provided by the national government to ensure the successful implementation of the programs, in addition to financial support.

Politics had no role in the selection of Kampung for C-KIP investment. The selection was done solely on the basis of objective criteria. KIP had received different types of support from the ITS since 1976. Now the Kampung mapping required under C-KIP was done by the ITS, through its students. The social mapping helped the city government to take decisions about the programs to implement in each Kampung.

Thus, it can be said that C-KIP was a success because it adopted the strategy of involving the community people in the planning and implementation of its programs in each Kampung. The participatory planning process created a sense of ownership among the community people that motivated them not only to get involved in the planning process but also to mobilize funds, with their own resources, to supplement the city government's resources. Finally, the active involvement of the community people ensured the successful implementation of C-KIP's plans. Thus, it was C-KIP's community-driven development that brought a new dimension to the urban slum improvement programs (Dhakal 2002).

Baan Mankong: Secure Housing in Thailand

Many successful slum development initiatives were carried out through a partnership between the Government and the urban poor, through their community-based organizations. The process started in 1980, in Thailand, when the Thai government started providing support to projects for building houses and providing land for the urban poor. Among different projects, there was a "land-sharing" scheme through which the Government provided security of tenure and built infrastructure only when the poor expressed their positive intent to share the property on which they lived with the landowner. For this project, the government of Thailand instituted the Urban Community Development Office in 1992, with the authority to provide support, through loans, to community organizations that would aspire to build new housing, upgrade their old housing and start income-generating activities. Later, in 2000, the Community Organizations Development Institute (CODI) was formed, merging the Urban Community Development Office and the Rural Development Fund. This CODI was entrusted with the responsibility for the implementation of a national project with a goal to upgrade and secure tenure for 300,000 urban slum households, in 2000 poor communities, in 200 Thai cities, over five years (Archer 2012; CODI 2014).

In continuing the Thai government's original project, from 1980, through CODI, two new projects were finalized for reaching 1 million poor households with low income in five years. Among these two projects, the first was the *Baan Mankong* (secure housing) while the other was *Baan Ua Arthorn* (we care). The CODI was the implementation agency for *Baan Mankong*, providing infrastructure subsidy and housing construction credit to the underprivileged groups who applied for such assistance. Under *Baan Ua Arthorn*, the National Housing Authority was given the responsibility to design, construct and sell ready-to-occupy flats and houses to poor people at a subsidized rate. The eligible families were those who could pay US$ 25–37 per month in a "rent-to-own" payment scheme (Angel and Boonyabancha 1988; Boonyabancha 2005).

Baan Mankong used to provided financial support to the community organization while networks, formed and managed by the community's people, would work with stakeholders, including local governments, professional bodies, universities and NGOs, to conduct investigations in their locality to decide which poor people for whom to apply to CODI or the National Housing Authority for assistance. After investigation, these networks started designing projects to improve the conditions of the selected poor families within three to four years.

Upon completion of the plans, the funds for the infrastructure subsidies and housing loans were transferred directly to the groups so that community-managed programs could be implemented under their supervision. The CODI and UCDO have been practicing the empowerment of community-based organizations for the improvement of slum dwellers' housing since 1992. One of the main objectives of this program was to increase the capacity of poor people to work collectively with fellow members of their community. The project worked in the slum communities that had already built their houses by investing a large amount. In such cases, the support was provided from the project for the upgradation of these houses. If any community felt the need to relocate, the project searched for a nearby site in order to make sure that they were not required to pay a lot for land (Boonyabancha 2001).[2]

In order to empower the urban poor communities, their networks, and stakeholders in designing their own projects, the program tried to impose as few regulations as possible. Of course, it was quite difficult to administer a program in which the urban communities would be empowered to steer their own planning and implementation as well as build local partnerships, so that the whole city could get involved in the process of solution of an important problem (Boonyabancha 2001, 2005).

Ten pilot projects were implemented in 2003 in order to assess whether these housing schemes could become a national program to be upscaled nationwide. The preconditions for pilot projects were: (i) strong organizational capacity (ii) working experience with a different organization, and (iii) existence of families whose monthly income was below 10,000 baht or US$205 (at the currency rate prevailing then). For the pilots, those communities were selected that had already been organized and had a working relationship with other organizations and the housing schemes. Implementation was simplified by the fact that eight of the projects were on State-owned land.[3]

Achievements of the Program

Table 5.1 shows the achievements of the project, at various levels, up to 2005. Apart from the implemented projects, the preparation of the implementation of 415 new projects, in communities with around 3,00,000 households and 140 cities, were undergoing at the same time. Tables 5.2 and 5.3 depict the progress of the program, of projects that were implemented and the achievement in improving land tenure security.

[2] The project first implemented its activities in 1500 units of ten communities in 2003 and they also prepared to work in 20 cities. In 2004, they upgraded 15,000 units in 174 slums in 42 cities and finalized the preparation for further implementation in 50 cities. During this time, the project also provided support in different types of learning initiatives and establishing linkage with the city authorities. During 2005–2007, the project upgraded 285,000 units in 200 cities (Boonyabancha 2005).

[3] The six projects that attained great success were (i) land purchase and re-blocking, (ii) post-fire reconstruction and building a long-term base, (iii) relocation to nearby land, (iv) scaling up pilot projects, (v) land sharing, and (vi) the relocation of mini squatters on a long-term lease (Boonyabancha 2005).

Table 5.1 Progress for Baan Mankong; January 2003 to September 27, 2005

Total number of projects approved	304 projects
Number of districts and cities where the program is underway	140 cities and districts in 57 provinces (out of 76 total provinces in Thailand)
Number of districts/cities where projects have been *approved*	106 districts and cities in 53 provinces
Number of communities involved *(in approved projects)*	415 communities
Number of households *(in approved projects)*	29,054 households
Total budget approved: • Infrastructure upgrading grants • Housing and land purchase loans	1. US$ 25.7 million 2. US$ 14.4 million

Source: Boonyabancha (2005)

Table 5.2 Different kinds of projects

Types of upgrading projects supported by Baan Mankong (as of September 25, 2005)	*Number of projects*	*Number of families*	*Percentage (%)*
On the same site *(includes in situ upgrading, in situ reblocking or reconstruction, and land sharing)*	269	22,151	76
Nearby relocation (within 2 kms)	40	2109	7
Relocation (farther than 2 kms)	105	4784	16.5
Shelter house for homeless	1	100	0.5
Total	415	29,054	100

Source: Boonyabancha (2005)

Many lessons have been learned from the implementation of the *Baan Mankong* for slum improvement in other countries:

1. The program was implemented countrywide, ensuring the participation of the urban poor and community-based organizations that helped the development of ownership among the people.
2. Urban poor organizations, along with their local development partners, played the lead role during the upgrading pilot initiatives.

Table 5.3 The kinds of land tenure security improvement achieved by the projects

Status of land tenure after project	*Number of projects*	*Number of families*	*Percentage (%)*
Cooperative land ownership	158	9849	34
Long-term lease to community cooperative	171	14,897	51
Short-term lease to community cooperative *(less than 5 years)*	32	2282	8
Permission to use land	54	2062	7
Total	415	29,054	100

Source: Boonyabancha (2005)

3. The urban poor groups were given the freedom to make any sorts of changes in the final projects they wanted, based on their learning and experience gained through perceiving changes in the pilot projects.
4. We have observed the development of a new horizontal power structure due to the practice of horizontal linkage among different peer groups.
5. The Government did not consider slums as a deviation from the mainstream. Instead, they were considered to be a normal part of the city. Thus, people living in slums did not consider themselves as excluded groups.
6. Once people are given the responsibility to carry out massive development initiatives city-wide and nationwide, incapacity is a real possibility: what succeeds in a local neighborhood may not succeed to the same extent if it becomes a nationwide plan.
7. Inexperienced community people could make a project a great success by making a difference in implementation.
8. All residents, no matter how poor, have a role to play in the collective implementation of slum upgrading.
9. Implementing slum upgrading can unbridle the community's creativity and restore the culture of collective work.
10. Constructing a number of drains and roads is not the ultimate goal of upgrading urban poor communities. The development of rela-

tionships within and among communities and their collective efforts in ensuring the smooth implementation of an initiative is at least as important as building infrastructure.

11. Even poor people can save and these savings can be accumulated from the community, with credits distributed in a way, and the community has the capacity to ensure better management of finance and the upgrading process.
12. The true purpose of slum upgrading is building integrated community-driven development in cities where slums are located.

From these lessons, we can offer the following advice to slum-upgrading policy designers:

1. Land should be as a collective, not an individual asset.
2. Finance should be seen as a symbol of collective activism.
3. People involved in a collective financial system should take decisions collectively.
4. In order to gain success in the implementation of a social welfare program, a sense of ownership needs to be created among the community people.
5. Engagement of people under an umbrella provides them with the power to collectively negotiate their demands with the formal power structure.
6. In the context of the implementation of such a slum-upgrading project, the management system should be vertical rather than horizontal.

Community Federations and City Upgrading: Pamoja Trust and Muungano in Kenya as Models

Bringing positive changes in the living standards of people in slums was the main task of the Pamoja Trust and Muungano of Kenya. In order to attain this objective, these organizations were carrying out advocacy to influence the Government to give support, mobilize the community, build a sense of ownership and raise funds from different sources and share learning with different stakeholders. It is worth noting that these organizations were implementing their projects in a precise social and political context (Weru 2004). The following discussion will provide an illustration of the sociopolitical history of Kenya, in which these organizations were implementing their programs for the upgrading of slums.

Muungano wa Wanvijiji

Muungano wa Wanvijiji was a foundation of the urban poor in Kenya. It started working as a community organization in partnership with many Kenya-based NGOs, Catholic priests and human rights activists. The main objective of this foundation was to fight against the Government's decision to evict slum dwellers from their slums. The foundation emerged based on the outcome of a series of dialogues and workshops that were arranged by the Mazingira Institute, which was an NGO based in Nairobi. The initial intention of the foundation was to work for the grant of land rights. Then, the community organizers of the foundation established linkages with different federations of urban poor people from India and South Africa. Based on their association with these foundations, they felt the need to build a community organization (Weru 2004).

Pamoja Trust

With an aim to strengthen and support urban poor community organizations, the Pamoja Trust was established in 2000. Basically, this organization was working to ensure access of the urban poor to land, shelter and services. In order to attain this objective, they started accumulating their own savings and introduced loan schemes that they managed by themselves. Through engaging community leaders, they introduced the leaders to a different role. Although there were many conflicts among the community people during the initial phases of the creation of the foundation, they became successful in overcoming those conflicts through greater community engagement. Considering the Trust as a potential threat to the local power structure, the Government forcefully tried to destroy the Trust and arrested many community organizers. But, the Trust continued their work, receiving assistance from a number of Nairobi-based international NGOs, including MISEREOR (the German international NGO) and the Maryknoll priests of Oxfam (Weru 2004).

Background of Slum Development

Urban poor housing in Nairobi was below standard despite the city's international exposure as the gateway of East Africa, even as the city hosted the offices of many international organizations. In 1995, more than half of the inhabitants of the city were living in slums that were informal and illegal. These illegal settlements comprised one-twentieth of Nairobi's total area (Alder 1995). The poor living conditions in these settlements resulted in a very high infant and child mortality rate in the city (APHRC 2002). These settlements were congested without basic infrastructure that made them vulnerable to fires (Weru 2004).

Due to the existence of serious conflicts among the landowners and occupants, and battles among diverse traditional groups, many organizations found it quite difficult to implement any projects to improve the situation of the informal settlements in Nairobi. Although these lands did not have authorized tenancy rights, there were landowners ("construction owners") and occupants with different priorities. There was a tug-of-war between the two groups where the landlords aspired to obtain land title for their structures and tenants demanded title to the land where they lived. Among the landlords, there were some rich people who earned a lot of money through renting a large number of huts. During the early days of independence, the Kenyan government implemented a policy of destroying all informal settlements in the city despite the fact that the poor urban population did not have any alternative housing. The process started in 1963 and continued into the 1970s. However, the Government changed their approach in the 1980s and, after that a minimum number of settlements were destroyed. The Government again reversed this policy in 1990 and demolished two large settlements, called Muoroto and Kibagare, which dislodged around 30,000 people living in these slums. In 1992, when partisan politics returned to Kenya, the intensity of demolition was reduced. However, President Daniel Arap Moi's Government evicted thousands of urban poor people by demolishing many urban settlements. This policy ended when Moi was ousted from the office of the president in 2001 (Weru 2004).

The majority of the NGOs, after 1991, remained concentrated on trying to stop the demolitions of informal settlements, to save thousands of slum dwellers from the threat of eviction in Nairobi. For example, *Kituo Cha Sheria* (literally meaning "Centre For Justice"), which was a national NGO, fought for the urban poor who were under threat of illegal eviction, through filing court cases under the Public Interest Litigation Act. They asked the courts for temporary injunctions to stop the evictions until the court could decide their legality. They also advocated establishing a relationship between the poor people living in these settlements and the State. However, their views were rejected by a number of NGOs and community-based organizations that opposed any partnership with the Government. Since they did not build capacity at the local level, their initiatives could not be successful in the improvement of the living conditions of the poor.

During the latter part of the 1990s, eviction and demolition took place often in Nairobi. Along with demolition, corruption and repression by the police and local powerholders also increased. Thus, the life and livelihood of slum dwellers were restricted as they required the permission of the "leaders" in order to do anything. They were not even allowed to be on the street or build their huts. Thus, any organization wanting to work for the improvement of the living conditions of the poor found it quite difficult due to the power of the leaders (Weru 2004).

NGOs and their networks could reduce the amount of demolition. They could not do much good for the living conditions of the poor. Accordingly, there were street battles between the Government and the organizations for the poor at demolition and eviction sites in the slums. Another significant issue was the low-income communities that were isolated from one another and could not work together, nor could their NGOs as they lived in different places. Thus, the NGOs did little good and could not build community organizations or take political or legal action of a permanent sort, but only lead street action or use the courts to try to keep things from getting worse.

Saving Groups

After the year 2000, Kenyan NGOs began to follow a model of collective savings developed in many areas of the world. NGO members or workers would collect money from individuals, either for savings or repayment of loans, every day, which also built relationships with, and gave information to, the slum residents. The NGOs used this to develop policy proposals that they then pushed the local authorities to act on. Beyond helping slum residents to save, the NGOs also helped them to buy land or used contributions for political action (Weru 2004).

During the early phase of the saving programs, 100 groups were formed with 10,000 members in 60 settlements in Nairobi. The number of saving groups almost doubled during 2002. Later on, 54 schemes were able to frame their constitutions by 2002, while 43 schemes opened bank accounts and appointed collectors. There was a positive competition for savers among different savings groups. The groups did not work through the Pamoja Trust, so no one knew how many there really were (Weru 2004).

Saving groups (Weru 2004) (a) organized members of the community and mobilized finances, (b) created networks and unity among the communities with the expectation that they would be able to deal with their own resources and implement their own development plans, (c) carried out activities with the expectation that the communities would be able to share and disseminate information about their daily activities, (d) empowered the community to fight poverty without seeking assistance from others, (e) supported residents when they procured services and got access for them to loans and credits, (f) empowered the community to make decisions about the spending of their money collectively, and (g) provided training to increase members' skills in management enhancing their self-confidence and negotiation skills, with the expectation that they would handle different development activities, including housing, procurement and services and management of resources.

Exchanges

In order to create opportunities for learning from others, exchange visits were organized so that each group would learn from the best practices of other groups. In most cases, the visits were organized locally, meaning that one slum's organizations would visit another slum's organizations in Nairobi, although sometimes intercity exchange visits were organized. The main purpose of the exchange visits was to learn from others, but it was also organized with an intention to build harmony among different groups, so that they could network and share information. This network created personal as well as community bonds that helped the organizations to collect and preserve their individual and collective strengths to advance their interests.

In 2002, a total of 32 local exchange visits in 41 communities were organized to strengthen saving schemes. These exchange visits were supported by the Pamoja Trust. During this time, a total of 18 intercity exchange visits were also organized, which were supported by the Pamoja Trust funds. Pamoja Trust and *Muungano* also arranged ten international exchange visits to Uganda, at the invitation of the Government of Uganda, which sought ideas for strategies to help their own urban poor communities. On one of the visits, a Memorandum of Understanding was signed between the Government of Uganda, the UK charity Homeless International and Slum Dwellers International (Weru 2004). These exchange visits were beneficial for the participants for the following reasons:

1. As part of the visits, different communities found an opportunity to share their problems and challenges with the residents of other slums. Moreover, the community group members received support from the federation to set up a network with local, regional and other federations of slum dwellers around the world.
2. The communities were encouraged to share their information and experiences, to acquire knowledge from one another and understand how to operate similar activities and solve similar problems.
3. Physical participation and interaction with different communities provided an opportunity to gain experience in daily collection of savings.
4. Such visits created a sense of collectivism among the members. This allowed them to ask one another for help when they required assistance.
5. Such visits also encouraged communities to confront challenges more carefully.

Modelling and Commencement of the Construction of Houses

After years of struggle, the construction of houses only started in 2003 in Nairobi. Engaging the tenants and structure owners, the measurement of land was completed and an agreement was reached on the distribution of houses once they were built. In addition to these, other issues including planning, appropriate design and arrangement of finance and loans were also considered before the commencement of the construction.

Among five settlements in Huruma, a permanent structure was built in Ghetto in 2002. Before an agreement was reached on the modelling of houses, discussions were held among the community members in order to accommodate the needs of all the slums. For instance, after the discussion, it was decided that slum dwellers would require small plots in order to accommodate all of them in the new structures. Accordingly, layouts of the sites were developed, accommodating all the households. As regards the finance required for the construction of new houses, the community members individually and collectively contributed to the mobilization of funds, making provision for external audits of the finances.

Among the five communities that completed their modelling of housing, only one had funds to commence construction from their own money. Therefore, they started their construction after providing training to their community members, who would help them in carrying materials of construction. Later on, the Nairobi City Council agreed to provide funds for all 39 houses in Hurima to start their construction.

One important issue was that tenants would require alternative housing, as their existing houses would be demolished first to build their new houses. Another issue was: who would provide the labor for the construction of the community toilet? After deciding these issues, the construction of the housing started (Weru 2004).

Slum Development Program in Manila, Philippines

Manila's slum development efforts, from 1975, involved a greater investment than Jakarta's (US$83 per person in Manila, US$60 in Jakarta, in 1975 dollars). Manila focused on the Tondo slum, occupied by about 200,000 squatters. Keare and Paris' (1983) evaluation was that Tondo was greatly improved by 1981. Housing had been improved. The settlement was less damaging to the environment. Small businesses had revived. There were more recreational facilities available. Transport had been improved. There were better health facilities. Families were more stable and the community was more cohesive.

However, by the 1990s, Tondo, like Calcutta and Jakarta, had reverted to its previous condition. In 1992, only seven of the public toilets built in the 1980s, with World Bank assistance, were in good working order or required only minor repairs (Luna et al. 1994: 1–2). More than one-third of the water supply had been siphoned off through leaks or by illegal tapping, leading to low water pressure, supply interruption, and extensive flooding. According to a World Bank report (Bartone et al. 1994: 92–94), all of Metropolitan Manila's surface water contained some human, solid and industrial wastes. A 1000 tons of solid waste was left uncollected each day. One of the worst urban air pollution records among the major world cities capped the misery of life in Metro Manila.

A Twin-Track Approach

It will be difficult enough to meet the need to raise living standards in the slums of today. Yet, if we do not plan to prevent the slums of tomorrow, our action will have only a temporary effect. This is what Tondo proves. A twin-track approach is therefore necessary. *First*, we must consider how stakeholders in today's slums—the poor, national and local governments, civil society groups, the private sector, and the international community—relate and can relate. *Second*, we need to develop methods to combine the strengths of stakeholders to maximize synergies.

The first issue in every slum is a livelihood. The poor, especially the very poor, need either to live within walking distance of their livelihood or have access to free transport to get to it. Turner (1967) and Payne (2005) pointed out that this is more important than the security of tenure or formal credit. If you cannot work, you cannot pay rent or repay loans. Yet livelihood is most easily acquired in wealthy areas where the cost of land is high. To make the slum dwellers self-sufficient, they need to be given land free or at a low or nominal cost. This gives them an asset that they can use to acquire funds for their businesses. Yet the cost of such a strategy would be too high for most third-world governments: they would have to buy the most expensive land in the cities and give it away. Even worse, experience shows that such a solution encourages the poor to sell their lands, realize a quick profit and then go back to the slums, hoping to get another such house. A more-economical solution is free transport: providing free public transport to slum dwellers for employment or business outside the slums. Work in desirable areas means that slum dwellers become literal importers of money to the slum, which they can use to upgrade their housing and amenities in the slums. Still, the security of tenure is important, especially to families with children. There are many options: a relocation/eviction moratorium; temporary occupation licenses; communal or individual leases; community land trusts; communal ownership; customary tenure, etc. The duration of tenure may be short or long, depending on what stakeholders in slum land can be convinced to accept. Over time, slums could be extended or upgraded in the official land tenure system, through introducing the system of providing incenses or leases or providing allocation for investment as a mechanism. These alternatives could be thought of in order to provide the slum people rights to the land they are occupying so that they could access many services provided by the municipal government.

Attention needs to be paid to eliminating the opportunity of the more-affluent in the community to buy slum land. Such "gentrification" creates beautiful, trendy suburbs where slums used to be but leaves the community the problem of permanently and hopelesslyhomeless poor people who quickly drink up their windfall profits. A high tax on capital-gains from purchase or sale—on both the gentrifier and the gentrified—of slum land could accomplish this, especially if the revenues were invested in new houses and land, or livelihood training and capital, for displaced victims of gentrification. These measures can be supplemented by a revision or elimination of administrative regulations that raise the cost of entry to legal shelter (Payne 2001).

Better transport, better security of tenure and discouraging gentrification is Track 1. Track 2 in a two-track approach is reducing the future causes of slums. To some extent, Track 1 will produce Track 2: slum dwellers transported out of the slums for livelihood (and young people transported out for better education) will upgrade their housing and amenities in the slum, putting the slum on an upward path to development and reducing the likelihood that it will fall back into being a hopeless slum. Security of tenure will reduce the likelihood of the success of current residents being disrupted by new generations of squatters. Ending gentrification will stop the chasing of poor people from one slum area to another. Yet these collateral benefits will help at the margin, not substitute for real Track 2 action.

To prevent the development of slums, we need to understand why poor people prefer to live there. The root causes are the local government's urban planning framework that raises the cost of and delays the construction of buildings. Regrettably, the bureaucratic procedures in relation to planning and implementation restrict the progress of upgrading the condition of slums. De Soto (1989), in his notable work, mentions that the finalization of the legalization of informal settlements in Lima had to travel through 59 bureaucratic steps that took around 20 years. A similar experience was reported by Struyk et al. (1990), who noted that the issuance of a land title in West Java took around 32.5 months. The lengthy process of the titling increased the cost of land acquisition by around 10–29%. Similar experiences on the procedural tangle of urban planning law were observed in different countries. The bureaucratic procedures discouraged the involvement of the private sector in the process of meeting the needs of the lower-income households. Reservation of land, for roads and other public purposes, was also another important factor that increased the cost of land, and thus of building. The demand for land in the cities of Europe was higher than for land in the cities of developing countries. The capital cost of this land was also quite high, along with the maintenance costs, which were being paid by the local authorities. As McAuslan (1989: 30) noted in the case of Chennai (previously Madras), India:

> *…so concerned have the authorities been to close every loophole against illegal development, corruption, exploitation of scarce resources, the exercise, and therefore the possible wrongful or non-exercise, of discretion, that the principal aim of the Madras Metropolitan Development Authority—to get orderly and equitable development underway in Madras and its environs—has been lost sight of.* (McAuslan 1989: 30)

McAuslan (1989) was of the opinion that the domination of political elites was evident in the process of identifying the needs and interests of the poor. Such domination could influence poor people to live—or to be put—far away from richer people.

With increased free markets in recent years, urban planning sticks out as one of the least deregulated of economic activities. Often the regulations are old and inefficient. Payne and Majale (2004), in their research on six countries, found similar facts. They concluded that regulatory frameworks were the main hindering factors that create problems for poor and middle-income households seeking to access their legal rights. The State must not protect people out of having any homes of their own and thus perhaps different standards are needed in rich and poor suburbs. Yet, if

State or local government planning were so efficient, there would be no slums, as slums fail to meet any conceivable standard of human habitation that a local government might create.

Applying New Approaches in Cambodia

Cambodia is an example of the twin-track approach to slum development argued for here. A project supported by Cities Alliance, GTZ and UN-Habitat, in 2003–2004, wanted to intensify the security of tenure for people living in slums in Phnom Penh, while also facilitating their access to affordable, legal housing in new developments. Previous research in Cambodia supported the necessity of both security of tenure *in situ* and opportunities for access to better housing elsewhere.

After the Communist Khmer Rouge regime, which disbursed Phnom Penh's population around the country in 1975–1978, collapsed in early 1979, people returned to Phnom Penh and other urban centers. Whoever found an empty lot or empty house and liked it, took it and lived there. In January 1979, all existing titles and land documentation were nullified. Then some new occupiers registered their own titles but, in many cases, just continued to occupy land without title. The State also took a large proportion of Phnom Penh land for public purposes. A civil war in 1979–1993 caused many peasants to flee the fighting to Phnom Penh and other cities. They either squatted on empty land or shared dwellings with existing inhabitants. Even after the war, urban prosperity continued to attract the rural poor with job opportunities. So there were informal settlements of poor people everywhere in Cambodian cities—along roadsides, riversides, railway lines and even on the tops of apartment buildings. The military government of 1979–1993 reacted by sporadic evictions of these settlements, resettling occupants outside the cities with only basic amenities and little livelihood opportunities. Sometimes, the resettled slum dwellers sneaked back into other slums in the cities.

Thus, the first priority of the 2003–2004 project was to stop the evictions and provide security of tenure to the informal settlements in the cities. At the same time, a regulatory audit of State planning was conducted to find ways of reducing the costs of new legal housing developments. The audit found that the planning procedures and requirements were inherited from the French, when Phnom Penh was a backwater of French Indochina, from 1860 to 1955. The French vision of Phnom Penh was as a semirural provincial town, not a national capital, and seemed more targeted at creating open space for colonial villas than providing houses for peasants. Also, in keeping with much governance in France itself, the system was inaccessible, expensive, restrictive, bureaucratic, illogical, slow and inefficient.

So, most Cambodians were ignoring it. Most lands were simply, according to the French system, illegally occupied and used. Yet, in French civil law, an illegal occupant has no right of tenure, nor did the Cambodian Army care much about the rights of poor occupants if a settlement was in an inconvenient place. This was the root of the informal settlement problem in Cambodia. So the audit proposed to rewrite the planning law and regulations to encourage and make practical the legal ownership and use of land for housing for the poor.

Dharavi of India Mumbai, India

Dharavi, Asia's largest slum, lies on high-value land in the middle of India's financial capital, Mumbai (Bombay). Dharavi has a population of more than a million, many of whom are second-generation residents, born there.

Dharavi is a mass of narrow, dirty lanes, open sewers, and cramped huts. Rents in Dharavi are easily affordable for the poor and Mumbai's two main suburban rail lines, heavily subsidized for all passengers regardless of income, make it easy for Dharavi residents to get to livelihood anywhere in the metropolis. Even living in small single rooms, most residents have gas for cooking and reliable electricity supply. Many residents have color televisions with cable connections and video players: it is a twenty-first-century sort of poverty, poor on the outside and middle-class inside.

Small-scale, informal industry abounds in Dharavi, producing garments, leatherwork, pottery and plastic. The annual turnover of Dharavi business is estimated at more than \$650 m (£350 m) a year. The Maharashtra State Government plans to redevelop Dharavi as a modern township, with proper housing, shopping complexes, hospitals and schools, at a cost of \$2.1 billion (£1.1 billion) (Dharavi Slum in Mumbai, Retrieved from http://news.bbc.co.uk/2/shared/spl/hi/world/06/dharavi_slum/html/dharavi_slum_intro.stm, accessed on April 6, 2010).

The Rajiv-Indira Housing Society of Dharavi

The Rajiv-Indira Housing Society of Dharavi (R-IHSOD) was the first Slum Rehabilitation Authority (SRA) initiative that began working in 1999. The Society was led by community members themselves, in a three-way partnership of SPARC, *Dharavi Vikas Samiti* ("Dharavi Development Committee") and a housing society of the slum dwellers. Later, two other housing societies joined in. In 2000, Citibank became the first international bank in Mumbai that approved a loan for the housing of the poor, to implement the Society's project. Homeless International of Britain, an NGO, was a guarantor for this loan. R-IHSOD was Rs. 8.5 crore (just over $1.5 million) project. Five buildings were constructed. Among them, two were of five stories and three of seven stories. As required by the SRA, 217 slum families were given free 225 sq. ft. tenements, with all other tenements sold on the open market. Transfer of development rights generated a further profit (retrieved from https://pdfs.semanticscholar.org/cfed/f0fe652bb52594d409b07a06d63069ff7714.pdf, accessed on 23/12/2018).

Bharat Janata Cooperative Housing Societies

R-IHSOD was attractive to developers and purchasers of tenements because it was on the main road. Yet what could be done for dwellers in slums that were far from the main road, in places less desirable to market buyers, financiers and housing developers? The Bharat Janata Cooperative Housing Society acquired 2507 square meters, in the centre of a slum, far from the main road, to build new housing for its members. The development consisted of five ground-plus-seven-story buildings—two for rehabilitation units, one for-sale unit and two a mix of for-rehabilitation and for-sale units. It was agreed that all 142 households would receive a 225 sq. ft. unit each for their rehabilitation, as their houses were demolished for the construction of the new buildings. In addition to these, 14 more rehabilitation units were also reserved for persons who were willing to evacuate their plots for the construction of toilet blocks or other developments in Dharavi. Under the construction plan, three places were dedicated to a welfare centre, community hall and *balwadi*.[4]

[4] *Balwadi* is an Indian preschool run for economically weaker sections of society, either by the State or by NGOs (Shukla 2004).

The BJCHS project is in an area more typical of the Dharavi slum than was the R-IHSOD. If this project works, it will offer a model for rehousing of far more Dharavi residents. Also, this project, if successful, proves the hypothesis that flats can be sold even to people from neighboring slums.

Other Examples from India

The National Slum Development Program (NSDP) was launched by the Federal Government in 1996 with a budget of Rs. 400 crores ($ 4 billion) per year. NSDP provides physical amenities, community infrastructure, health care and social amenities to slum communities, plus 10% of the total budget for housing construction or improvement, released to State and Territory Governments in proportion to their percentage of the national slum population. It is the responsibility of the Neighborhood Committees and Community Development Societies to execute the NSDP locally. The implementation-related activities were supervised by the Slum Development Committees that included elected representatives from ULBs, NGOs, and community-based organizations. The program contains both the loan and subsidy components. The loan amount accounts for 70%, while the subsidy accounts for 30% in larger States; 90% of amount is allocated as subsidy as opposed to 10% as loan in the small States. It is the contractors who execute all the implementation-related activities (Buckley et al. 2007). *Valmiki Ambedkar Awas Yojana* (*VAMBAY*), which commenced in 2001, builds housing for the urban poor, including sanitation facilities, which have an earmarked 20% share of grants to States. Rs 3 billion per year are given to State agencies, who choose beneficiaries and give them the land title or license rights. Then beneficiaries can avail of grants through HUDCO loans and matching subsidies (the State must provide 50%) to build or upgrade their houses through contractors. The target population is urban slum dwellers below the poverty line or in economically weaker sections (Buckley et al. 2007).

Urban Ashraya Housing Program is a Government of Karnataka State's scheme to provide 300,000 urban and 800,000 rural housing units to poor households that are homeless. Urban households can receive grants of Rs. 25,000–40,000, with land, but must contribute Rs. 5000 to build their homes. Beneficiaries are chosen from a 1995 survey of homeless persons, periodically updated by local councils (Buckley et al. 2007).

Mythri Housing Scheme was a Government of Kerala State's housing scheme that was implemented from 1996 to 2002; 270,000 homes were built under the scheme with financial assistance from the Kerala State Housing Board. A public–private modality was followed during the implementation of the process as the qualified beneficiaries received Rs 9000 each as a cash grant, while Rs 19,000 each was given as a loan. All the loans were allocated at a rate of 5.5% interest. Beneficiaries were poor persons who owned about 64 square meters of land and could contribute Rs. 2500 to build their homes (Buckley et al. 2007).

Conclusion

There have been many types and models of slum upgradation undertaken around the world. Some of these programs have become successful while others have failed. Among these programs, a number of programs are considered as best practices, as the rate of success of these programs is so great that different components of these programs are being replicated in other parts of the world. Among these programs, a number of best practices are Calcutta's Basti Improvement Program (BIP) and Dharavi in Mumbai in India, Comprehensive Kampung Improvement Program in Surabaya, Indonesia C-KIP Community Participation Model in Thailand, *Baan Mankong*: Secure Housing in Thailand, Kenya's Community Federation and City Upgradation: The Work of *Pamoja* Trust and *Muungano*, Slum Development program in Manila, Philippines, and the Twin-Track Approach, for example, in Cambodia, have attained a great amount of success in improving the situation of people living in slums. One of the driving factors that led these programs to attain a great deal of success was the adoption of the community development approach in the implementation of these programs. Through the involvement of the community people, the programs were successful in developing a sense of ownership by the community people, who started owning these programs even during the planning stage. That is why community people continued to take these programs ahead even after the initial project was terminated and ensured the sustainability of these programs. The subsequent chapter provides a discussion on the urban slum upgradation good practices in Bangladesh, with a focus on the major challenges and possible solutions.

References

Alder, G. (1995). Tacking poverty in Nairobi's informal settlements: Developing an institutional strategy. *Environment and Urbanization, 7*(2): 85–107.

Angel, S., & Boonyabancha, S. (1988). Land sharing as an alternative to eviction: The Bangkok experience. *Third World Planning Review, 10*(2), 107–127.

APHRC (2002). Population and health dynamics in Nairobi's informal settlements. Nairobi: African Population and Health Research Centre.

Archer, D. (2012). Baan Mankong participatory slum upgrading in Bangkok, Thailand: Community perceptions of outcomes and security of tenure. *Habitat International, 36*(1), 178–184.

Bartone, C., Bernstein, J., Leitmann, J., & Eigen, J. (Eds.). (1994). *Toward environmental strategies for cities.* Washington, DC: World Bank.

Boonyabancha, S. (2001). Savings and loans—Drawing lessons from some experiences in Asia. *Environment and Urbanization, 13*(2), 9–21.

Boonyabancha, S. (2005). Baan Mankong: Going to scale with "slum" and squatter upgrading in Thailand. *Environment and Urbanization, 17*(1), 21–46.

Buckley, R. M., Mahavir, S., & Jerry, M. (2007). Strategizing slum improvement in India: A method to monitor and refocus slum development programs. *Global Urban Development, 3*(1). Retrieved May 8, 2017, from http://www.globalurban.org/GUDMag07Vol3Iss1/Buckley.htm.

CODI. (2014). *Progress report of Baan Mankong.* Bangkok: Community Organisations Development Institute.

De Soto, H. (1989). *The other path: The invisible revolution in the Third World.* New York: Harper and Row.

Dhakal, S. (2002). Comprehensive Kampung Improvement Program in Surabaya as a model of community participation. *Working Paper.* Urban Environmental Management Project, Institute for Global Environmental Strategies (IGES), December 2002, Kitakyushu, Japan. Retrieved May 6, 2017, from www.iges.or.jp/en/ue/pdf/dhakal/dhakal_KAMPUNG.pdf.

Hiebeler, R., Kelly, T., & Ketteman, C. (1998). *Best practices: Building your business with customer-focused solutions.* New York: Simon & Schuster.

Keare, D. and Paris, S. (1983). Evaluation of shelter projects for the urban poor. Washington, DC: World Bank.

Keehley, P., Medlin, S., MacBride, S., & Longmire, L. (1997). *Benchmarking for best practices in the public sector: Achieving performance breakthroughs in Federal, State, and Local Agencies.* San Francisco: Jossey-Bass Inc. Publishers.

Luna, E. M., Ferrer, O. P., & Ignacio, U., Jr. (1994). *Participatory action planning for the development of two PSF projects.* Manila: University of Philippines.

McAuslan, P. (1989). *Land law, tenure and registration issues and options.* Paper presented at the Urban Land Development Seminar, World Bank, Washington, DC.

Ostrom, E., Schroeder, L. D., & Wynne, S. G. (1993). *Institutional incentives and sustainable development: Infrastructure policies in perspective*. Boulder, CO: Westview Press.

Øyen, E. (2004). Poverty production: A different approach to poverty understanding. In N. Genov (Ed.), *Advances in sociological knowledge*. Wiesbaden: VS Verlag für Sozialwissenschaften.

Payne, G., & Majale, M. (2004). *The urban housing manual: Making regulatory frameworks work for the poor*. London: Earthscan.

Pugh, C. (1990). *Housing and urbanisation*. New Delhi: Sage.

Payne, G (2001). Lowering the ladder: Regulatory frameworks for sustainable development. *Development in Practice, 11*(2/3): 08–318.

Payne, G. (2005). Getting ahead of the game: A twin-track approach to improving existing slums and reducing the need for future slums. Environment and Urbanization, 17: 135–145.

Retrieved April 6, 2010, from http://news.bbc.co.uk/2/shared/spl/hi/world/06/dharavi_slum/html/dharavi_slum_intro.stm.

Retrieved December 23, 2018, from https://pdfs.semanticscholar.org/cfed/f0fe652bb52594d409b07a06d63069ff7714.pdf.

Senge, P. (1990). *The fifth discipline: The art and practice of learning organizations*. Garden City: Doubleday.

Shukla, R. P. (2004). *Early childhood care and education* (p. 106). New Delhi: Sarup & Sons.

Sivaramakrishnan, K. C. (1994). *Urban environmental governance*. Washington, DC: The World Bank.

Struyk, R., Hoffman, M., & Katsura, H. (1990). *The market for housing in Indonesian cities*. Washington, DC: The Urban Institute Press.

Thomas, F. C. (1997). *Calcutta poor*. Armonk, NY: M. E. Sharpe.

Turner, J. F. C. (1967). Barriers and channels for housing development in modernizing countries. *Journal of the American Institute of Planners, 33*(3), 67–81.

Werlin, H. (1999). The slum upgrading myth. *Urban Studies, 36*(9), 523–1534.

Weru, J. (2004). Community federations and city upgrading: The work of Pamoja Trust and Muungano in Kenya. *Environment and Urbanization, 16*(1), 47–62.

CHAPTER 6

Urban Slum Upgrading Best Practices in Bangladesh

Introduction

People usually migrate from rural to urban areas (towns and cities) because they have to, not because they want to. The growing number of landless households and lack of job opportunities in rural areas make these areas less and less livable. Rural people, who have always been poor, lack even land and a home of their own to live in. They come to the cities with nowhere to go, having no land there either. Lacking money for rent of quality living space, rural refugees live in the slums. Even basic amenities, like water supply, sanitation, waste collection or infrastructure are lacking in slums. Disease, crime and natural disasters are, therefore, commonplace in slums. Governments, NGOs and donor countries have carried out projects to upgrade the living conditions of the people in slums and to reduce poverty in slums. This chapter discusses some of the most successful community projects to improve living conditions for slum dwellers since the start of this millennium.

Slum-Upgradation Strategies

Massive urbanization and increasing urban poverty, which began in the 1960s, have been the most obvious trends in the cities of developing countries. Rapid urban population growth, with the arrival from rural areas of people with lower and lower average incomes, has been the root of many problems. Many rural arrivals in cities wind up living illegally,

P. K. Panday, *The Face of Urbanization and Urban Poverty in Bangladesh*, https://doi.org/10.1007/978-981-15-3332-7_6

"squatting" on lands without the owners' permission. Slums are thus a problem of most cities in the developing nations. Generally, there are three strategies to address the problem of slums: (i) slum clearance, (ii) slum relocation, and (iii) slum upgrading (Islam 1997).

Slum clearance proceeds on the assumption that both slums and their occupants are a problem. This thinking is fueled, especially among local governments, by the fact that the slum housing is illegal: either the dwellers have no right to be there or the housing does not comply with building standards. Therefore, the strategy is to eliminate the slums, using bulldozers, fire, and other means. Residents are removed, the land is cleared and new buildings, up to modern standards of amenities, are constructed. High-rise buildings often replace low-rise, substandard housing but population density does not actually increase. Yet the high-rise buildings lack the empty ground that low-income families need to earn their livelihoods through informal trade (Islam 1997). Thus, slum clearance often leads to areas that are neater, cleaner, more modern and poorer. Also, wholesale demolition and reconstruction literally "from the bottom up", while providing temporary resettlement for occupants, is a very costly solution.

Slum relocation usually implies removing slum dwellers from the urban areas to purpose-built housing in rural or semi-urban areas. Then the problem is livelihood. Rural people come to cities because their larger populations provide a larger market for trade and there are more employment opportunities, even at low wages. Back in the rural areas after relocation, the ex-slum dwellers are actually poorer, as they have no options to earn income. Consequently, slum relocation is usually not an advisable practice unless removal is necessary for the residents' safety: as in the case of fire or natural disaster. In such cases, the State needs to provide rations to assure the daily needs of the relocated people. Then, slum relocation becomes a very expensive option, as governments have to spend for removal, accommodation, rations and transportation to employment and other amenities. For nonemergency slum intervention, there are usually better and cheaper alternatives to slum relocation.

Upgradation of slums refers to the improvement of the existing setup, including water reticulation, sanitation, clean drainage and electricity, up to a standard that satisfies its residents. Generally, upgradation means loans to improve infrastructure, which is less costly, in the long term, than infrastructure construction or destruction. Other actions that can be included in slum upgrading include remedying dangerous or polluting conditions, creating systems for community self-government and planning and provision of new amenities for transport, health care, education, power supply and sanitation. One of the important elements of slum upgradation is giving tenancy rights to slum dwellers so that they can legalize their places of accommodation at prices they can afford. Absentee landlords are not known as great caretakers of their properties but, given the resources, people always want to improve the accommodation that they own and live in. Some significant advantages of slum upgrading are reduced cost (as low as 10% of the cost of slum clearance or relocation), reduced disturbance to the livelihood and tranquility of the community: slum clearance and relocation is, by nature, traumatic and sometimes violent. The consequence of the slum upgradation must be observable and fast action that could improve the living standards of the poor people in urban areas positively.

Slum upgrading has been successfully used as a slum strategy many times in Bangladesh, by the State, local government and NGOs. It has usually proven to be the best slum strategy for the reasons stated above and is to be preferred in most circumstances.

Dushtha Shasthya Kendra (DSK): A Successful Example of Slum Upgrading in Dhaka, Bangladesh

Bangladesh Bureau of Statistics data indicates that about 25% of Bangladesh's population (about 35 million) lives in urban areas. By 2025, the urban proportion of Bangladesh's population will be greater than 50%. Slums are a big problem in Bangladesh's largest conurbations: Dhaka, Chittagong, Khulna, Rajshahi and Sylhet, in that order of magnitude. Poor housing, infrastructure, health and socioeconomic conditions are normal facts of life in Bangladesh's slums. The Slum Mapping and Census (2005) found that city taps were used by 62.7% of the slum population as a potential source of drinking water (a most unhealthy practice), while 33.4% and 3.8% used tube wells and sources like rivers, ponds, lakes and canals, respectively. One tap was shared with 6–10 families by 40.9% of slum dwellers, while in 22.7% of cases, 11–20 households shared a single tap (cited in Jinnah 2007).

In the past, households who owned no land in the city could not access city water. If they did not lease from a landlord, who could deal with the Dhaka Water Supply and Sewerage Authority (DWASA) directly for their water supply, the DWASA would not discuss the matter with landless people. DSK, a Dhaka-based nongovernmental organization (NGO), initiated the "DSK Initiative" to help slum dwellers access public water and sanitation services.

About 35% of Dhaka City residents live in slums. The thought of 35% of people in the capital city lacking access to a basic necessity of life like water is shocking enough. To address this issue, DSK, in partnership with WaterAid Bangladesh, made themselves the agents for slum dwellers and dealt with DWASA for their water and sewerage supply when DWASA refused to deal with the slum dwellers directly.

Only after months of persuasion did DSK succeed in getting DWASA to supply slum dwellers with water and sanitation. One strategy of DSK to obtain DWASA agreement to supply water to slum dwellers was to provide bond money, which gave DWASA security of payment for services that DWASA supplied to the slum residents.[1] Landless, penniless people make notoriously bad credit risks. DWASA had been afraid that they would have to give the water away for free because the slum dwellers could never pay them. As a consequence of DSK's intervention with bond money, two water points were approved by DWASA, in poor areas of Dhaka, in the years 1992 and 1994, respectively. Influenced by the success of these two initiatives, DSK made their initial role, as a surety, a model for arranging water supply for slum dwellers throughout Bangladesh. Thus, DSK turned beggars, who were thought not worth talking to, into respected water supply customers. Under DSK pressure, a pilot project was initiated by DWASA, on this model, in 12 more slum areas in Dhaka (Bold et al. 2010).

After dealing successfully with DWASA, DSK started negotiations with the Dhaka City Corporation (DCC) to set up sources of water in the streets. The DCC agreed to let DSK set up sources of water by building streets on the lands of the City Corporation. The UNDP–World Bank Water and Sanitation Programme, the Swiss Agency for Development and WaterAid Bangladesh supported the DSK's water point construction project in the form of kickoff loans, as well as technical support. The DSK also began the relationship between DWASA and probable customers in slums, by promotion and intermediation, and encouraged the City to change

[1] WASA's major concern with supplying water to slum dwellers was that they were not only poor but transient. They came and went from the slums whenever they wished, unlike the owner of a house. Essentially, the DSK provided the legal personhood and permanent office that the slum dwellers did not have. So, DWASA felt confident in dealing with DSK in place of the slum dwellers themselves. DSK, for its part, was satisfied, through discussions with the slum dwellers that they would pay for water supply if they were given reliable service (Jinnah 2007).

policies that made it difficult to supply water to the urban poor (Jinnah 2007).

DSK also implemented their projects with the slum groups to increase their capability to deal with sources of water, to get them to make regular payments for water and to ensure full recovery of capital costs by the DWASA. After 16 years of regular payments for water supply to the slums, DWASA issued a landmark decision in 2008, under which Community-Based Organizations (CBOs) would be permitted to submit their application for water connections by themselves, without the assistance of middlemen. Today, many slum residents in Dhaka have become esteemed clients of DWASA and the system has been replicated throughout Bangladesh. These community people, who were once excluded from availing water supply, have remained enthusiastically engaged in the preparation and usage of water sources and repayment schemes (Bold et al. 2010). Habib (2009) mentioned the following lessons learned from DSK acting as a mediator in the water supply process for the benefit of the slum dwellers:

1. Residents of slum communities can be respected customers of the water supply authorities if they are given the opportunity of availing water supply at low cost.
2. Access to utility services could be provided when they prove their ability to pay for them.
3. The time has come for the Government to initiate changes in existing laws to expedite the supply of amenities to the poor urban in urban areas.
4. NGOs could play an important role in organizing slum dwellers to pay for amenities.
5. If community members can arrange formal supply of services for payment, pilferage is eliminated, so State revenues rise.

Strategies for Capacity-Building

DSK sees its role as capacity-building, for slum communities and service providers, to have mutually successful relationships. To carry out this role, DSK:

- Forms CBOs and empowers them, through methods such as training, meetings. visitations, dialogue, lobbying, advocacy and networking
- Engages local government agencies as communication points to assure WATSAN (water and sanitation) services and also enhances their capacity through training, meetings, visits and dialogue
- Provides training on Orientation & Monitoring to the caretakers, half of whom are female and to local masons building the water points
- Creates linkages between communities and service providers in general, especially local government providers
- Facilitates empowerment of community-based local entrepreneurs, masons, suppliers, contractors, etc., involved in infrastructure construction, repair and maintenance
- Provides information to the communities and to other stakeholders

DSK Project Extent

DSK's goal is to assure that 15 Wards of Dhaka and Chittagong have sanitation and water supply, supplemented by improved hygiene practices as a result of other projects. This goal has been mostly achieved during the 3.5 years of the project's operation. Eventually, 55,000 families in 155 slums will have hygienic sanitation, safe water supply and hygiene education by 2010 (Habib 2009).

Slum Improvement Project (SIP): Another Winning Project in Slum Renewal

With financial assistance from UNICEF, the People's Republic of Bangladesh is carrying out a Slum Improvement Project (SIP) under the Local Government Engineering Department (LGED). The purpose of SIP is to improve the lives of slum dwellers by measures such as expansion of infrastructure, primary health care, credit provision, and women's empowerment. SIP commenced in 1985.

Initially, 57 slums from 5 medium-sized towns were chosen for the implementation of SIP. Having started the second phase, 40,000 women from 185 slums of 25 cities and towns were brought under the coverage of the project by 1994 (Menon n.d.). One of the notable features of SIP was its distinct emphasis on the role of women in the activities of the project and community development. Menon (n.d: 16–17) summarized the major components of SIP as:

- The Central Coordination Committee (CCC), coordinating Ministries in Dhaka.
- UNICEF and the city governments provided policy inputs, coordinated activities and controlled financial and technical matters.
- A project implementation office (PIO) was established at the Local Government Engineering Department (LGED) to act as a secretariat to the CCC.
- At the city level, Project Implementation Committees (PIC), were headed by the Municipal Chairperson, with representatives from the relevant departments, and with an engineer from the LGED as the Project Manager.

Limitations of the SIP

Slum communities did not have to spend their own money except to pay 500 Tk per tube well or toilet into a community fund, which would pay community workers when UNICEF ended their involvement. However,

- City governments and the LGED Ministry activities overlapped and competed to control SIP in the cities.
- The project expanded before it was truly ready to do so.
- The project did not remain community-controlled and became yet another State infrastructure project. SIP became financially unsustainable as costs were not recovered, communities did not really own the projects and maintenance of services was not provided for. SIP was not properly targeted and benefits went to persons with monthly incomes above 2000 Tk. The group formation, training and community planning processes were not properly established. Women in the communities never truly became equal participants in SIP projects (Menon n.d.: 18).

SIP: Lessons Learned

Menon (n.d.), in his study, identified the following lessons learned:

- Successful women's organizations were established.

- SIP upgraded the infrastructure of the slums, with improved walkways, adjacent streets, drains, latrines, tube wells, etc.
- SIP savings and credit projects sharply increased slum family incomes.
- SIP improved public health and sanitation in the slums through its consciousness-raising and community participation projects, so the frequency of diarrhea, respirational problems and scabies was reduced (Menon n.d.: 17).

With all its limitations, SIP made a positive difference in Bangladesh's slums, especially in public health, family income through micro-credit and women's empowerment. One of the major contributions of SIP was that it brought massive changes in the field of health and sanitation through raising the level of awareness of women living in slums. Through increased knowledge, they could practice safer sanitation behavior, which resulted in the reduction of disease. They were also successful in empowering women through their programs on savings and credit, where they used community engagement mechanisms. As a result of their interventions, they enhanced the position of women in families and communities (Menon n.d.).

The Integrated Food Security Program (IFSP): Overseas Development Aid that Worked

The Integrated Food Security Program (IFSP) was a five-year food security project funded by the USA's foreign aid legislation. IFSP consolidated previous American foreign aid projects in Bangladesh, such as the International Federation for Family Development (IFFD) flood-proofing and UPWARD. It also introduced a food and livelihood security service for slum dwellers, among other new projects. IFSP operated in most of the country's Districts with at least one service. The three strategic objectives (SOs) of IFSP were: to encourage and defend family income and community capital and assets (SO1); to increase health, hygiene and nutritional practices of susceptible groups (SO2); and to stimulate effective and sustainable institutional support systems (CARE, Bangladesh 2002).

Components of IFPS

The four main components of IFSP were: the Supporting Household Activities for Hygiene, Assets and Revenue (SHAHAR); Building Union Infrastructure for Local Government (BUILD); Flood Proofing Project

(FPP); and (iv) Disaster Management Program (DMP). The intent of the program was to draw on these aspects to create a holistic livelihood support base for each household included. In implementation, the focus was on insecure and vulnerable groups and the strategy was to partner with local governments and Bangladesh NGOs. The purpose of these focuses and strategies was to ensure sustainability after the project expired in 2004 (CARE, Bangladesh 2002).

Such a strategy was quite appropriate for intervention in slums, whose inhabitants often have many different needs. Urban poverty is a multidimensional problem. However, of the four projects, only SHAHAR really concerned the urban poor, which is the subject of this chapter, and therefore there is a focus on ISP. Other interventions concerned the rural areas and Union Parishads (rural local councils).

The Supporting Household Activities for Hygiene, Assets and Revenue (SHAHAR)

SHAHAR (Supporting Household Activities for Hygiene, Assets and Revenue)[2] focused on the cities ("*Shohor*" means "city" in Bengali). CARE, Bangladesh commenced its operation in July 1999 in Tongi, an industrial suburb of Dhaka, and in Jessore, a District capital near the Indian border to the west. Nabolok, an NGO, implemented the project in Tongi. By the end of the project, SHAHAR was operational in four urban areas, with 35,000 households being served. There were four main actions of SHAHAR:

1. Urban infrastructure (including drains, footpaths, earth filling and community latrines)
2. Health, hygiene and nutrition education
3. Community mobilization and institutional strengthening
4. Income generation

The project was evaluated for its effects on socioeconomic indicators; health and hygiene; nutrition and diet; and governance and social institutions of the areas involved. These activities of SHAHAR are summarized in Table 6.1:

[2] For more details about the SHAHAR project, please visit http://www.ifpri.org/dataset/bangladesh-2.

Table 6.1 Implementation strategies for the SHAHAR component

Areas	*Interventions*
Infrastructure	1. Reconstruction/construction of drains and canals 2. Reconstruction/construction of footpaths and access roads 3. Reconstruction/construction of community sanitation facilities 4. Reconstruction/construction of community water points 5. Raising plinth levels of HHs 6. Construction of community grounds
IGA	1. Formation of IGA group and savings group 2. Business plan preparation and distribution of credit among poor women 3. Skill training in IGA entrepreneurship 4. Vocational Training
Health, Hygiene and Nutrition	1. Formation of mother and child groups for health, hygiene and nutrition education 2. Community awareness initiatives through "courtyard sessions" on HHN 3. Promotion of homestead/rooftop gardening 4. Community waste removal schemes
Community mobilization	1. Development of local Community Resource Management Committees (CRMCs) 2. Creation of partnerships with PNGOs 3. Institutional support of paurashava 4. Exploring leverage areas for local advocacy to address land tenure security 5. Promotion of greater representation by vulnerable urban households in municipal and paurashava planning process

Sources: Adapted from CARE, Bangladesh (2002: 33)

Advancing Sustainable Environmental Health (ASEH): An NGO Project that Worked

Nabolok NGO initiated Advancing Sustainable Environmental Health (ASEH) project from November 2005. WaterAid–Bangladesh provided funding. The project that lasted for four years was executed in 95 slums of Wards 1, 3, 21, 22, 24, 25 and 31 in Khulna.

Priorities and Strategies

The strategy of the project was to organize the slum dwellers into community-based organizations to "defend" themselves and demand better services. The project served 45,062 people in 9403 families. Water and sanitation, using a software–hardware approach, was a priority. Other objectives included:

1. Awareness-building on health, hygiene and sanitation
2. Water and sanitation infrastructure
3. Sustainability, operation and maintenance of existing facilities
4. Participation of local government
5. CBOs and other stakeholders in project implementation

ASEH had the following components (Retrieved from http://www.nabolokbd.org/urban.htm; accessed on 7/12/2018):

1. *Capacity-Building of the Community-based Organization* (Situation Analysis, Awareness and Motivation, Training, Sharing session, Exposure Visit)
2. *Hygiene Promotion* (Courtyard Sessions with Female Adolescent & Child Community, Tea Stall sessions with tea shoppers; and Mosque- and Temple-based sessions with religious leaders
3. *Community Campaign* (Ward Rally, Ward Fair, Popular Theatre, Cleanliness Day)
4. *Water Supply* (Installation of Deep Tube wells, Installation of Shallow Tube wells, Connection of Tap Stands, Connection of Water-Points, Construction of Rain Water Harvesting System)
5. *Environmental Sanitation* (Construction of Single Pit Latrines, Construction of Twin Pit Latrines, Construction of Cluster Latrine Septic tank, Construction of Block Latrines, Construction of Cluster Latrine Pits, Construction of Child-friendly Latrines)
6. *Solid-Waste Management* (Collection of Waste from Community, Action Research for Biogas Plantation)
7. *School Sanitation* (School Selection, School Teacher's Orientation, Debate Competition Among School Students, Construction Of School Latrines, Installation of Deep Tube Wells)

8. *Advocacy and Networking with Local Government Institutions and Other Agencies* (Workshops, Seminars, Training, Dialogue Sessions, Exposure Visits)
9. *Research and Innovation* (Social Study, Publication, Social Action)
10. *Staff Capacity-Building* (Training, Exposure Visits)

Population Services and Training Centre (PSTC): Taking on the Country's Biggest Slum and Winning

Chon Para Bashtohara Punorbashon Kendro (generally known as "Chanpara slum"), is one of the largest urban slums in Bangladesh. Chanpara is located in Rupgonj, Narayanganj, about 6 km away from Dhaka city, and is 1 km^2. in area. The slum was established by the State in 1975, as a resettlement center for 5000 of Dhaka's landless families. Chanpara's population has increased to 7766 families, with a total population of 38,000. Most of the families' livelihood is low-wage, unskilled employment: day labor, rickshaw driving, small business, garments and factory work, driving, etc., with a few employed in the State or the formal private sectors. Housing is almost all 24 × 18 feet in area made with a clay or concrete floor, allocated to the family by the Government (Ahmed 2006). There were no amenities in Chanpara except electricity and some concrete roads.

Population Services and Training Centre (PSTC) was a water supply and sanitation project started in Chanpara in 2000. By June 2003, 10% of the population of Chanpara had received 38 tube wells and 114 pit latrines from PSTC. PSTC recovered 100% of the cost of sanitary latrines and tube wells except for administration expenses. However, hardcore and vulnerable groups were not targeted because (Ahmed 2006):

- All residents were considered to be poor, and thus homogeneous, by the PSTC.
- Most of the meetings for the community baseline survey were dominated by relatively vocal and well-off people. (The meetings were held during daytime when most of the truly poor had to work.)
- PSTC expected recipients to pay for services, which the hardcore poor and vulnerable could not do. (Some poor and vulnerable had been included in the project for hand tube well services but had to be excluded because they could not make installment payments or could not show that they owned the hardware.)

Local Partnerships for Urban Poverty Alleviation (LPUPAP)

LPUPAP started in 2000 with UNDP and DFID funding and was conducted by *United Nations Centre for Human Settlements* (UNCHS) and Local Government Engineering Department (LGED). LPUAP was a capacity-building project conducted in three cities and eight towns, using strategies of community action planning, capacity-building, micro-finance and vocational training to reduce poverty. The project served 600,000 poor people.

The main strategy of LPUPAP was to create community-based savings as a basis for creation of micro-enterprises, with community action planning to address pressing needs and capacity-building for communities and local government, where needed, to accomplish the project's objectives. LPUPAP was a success. The project was completed in 11 cities outside Dhaka. The components were:

1. *Community Development Fund (CDF)*: LPUPAP made contracts with communities for the building of fundamental infrastructural facilities and physical developments, such as sanitary latrines, hand tube wells, cemented paths, drains and lampposts.
2. *Poverty Alleviation Fund (PAF)*: LPUPAP gave communities funds for savings and micro-credit.
3. *Capacity-Building*: LPUPAP provided such services to local governments to make them more effective in addressing the needs of the urban poor.

However, GHK (2006) and Islam et al. (2006) criticized LPUPAP as ineffective in improving conditions for the extremely poor, in their evaluations. Therefore, in the second phase of LPUPAP, after 2007, funding was increased from \$18 to \$120 million and physical planning and improvements to housing, in addition to infrastructure, were included. Some new areas of Dhaka were added to the project.

Urban Partnerships for Poverty Reduction (UPPR): Building on Success

UPPR was a 2007 initiative of UNDP, UN-Habitat, DFID and the Government to build on the success of LPUPAP. The focus was on the female poor and extremely poor, using a strategy of capacity-building at the family level to increase income and assets. The strategies were:

1. Link the skills and knowledge of the poor with the needs of local businesses as a kind of employment exchange, then upskill the poor and provide apprenticeships to the young poor. A part of this strategy was to work with partners who were effective at assisting women to enter nontraditional employment.
2. Subsidize poor entrepreneurs with technology transfer and links to banks and micro-finance institutions. Subsidize "backyard production" of meat and vegetables by upskilling producers and assisting them with market access to make this a source of income as well as of food (retrieved from http://webapps01.un.org/nvp/frontend!policy.action?id=192; on 23/12/2016).

By encouraging "backyard production" of urban and peri-urban food and meat, the project helped community members improve their methods of production, added value to what they produced and improved their access to markets.

Secondary Towns Water Supply and Sanitation Sector Project (STWSSSP): Community-Driven Development, Steered by a Bank

STWSSSP was the Asian Development Bank's use of Community-Driven Development theory to expand water supply and sanitation in Bangladesh, by lending $41 million to a $71 million project, from 2006. STWSSSP provided water supply and sanitation amenities to 16 rural towns on a "demand- and performance-driven" basis. This approach was a reaction against the traditional provision of such services by the Ministries in Dhaka without regard to local needs or demands traditionally. In developing and implementation of sanitation improvements, including the construction of infrastructure, NGOs and CBOs participated and communities could participate in procurement for public works contracts valued at less than $10,000 (ADB 2009).

Slum Development by SHEVA—Centre for Women and Children's Welfare: NGOs Working Successfully with Slum Dwellers

SHEVA took a bank loan to convert temporary structures for 40 families into semipermanent row houses with paved access, good ventilation, separate sanitation, gas for cooking, a community training/meeting room and a covered lounge area. The landowner mortgaged the land and signed an agreement to fix rent for 5 years. Tenants got training on water/sanitation management, skills development, health care, functional education, and were organized into a self-regulating community. The USD20,000 project cost was paid for in 7.5 years, at 12.5% interest. Tenants' rent doubled. Neighboring residents were asking to have similar projects for them (retrieved from http://www.shevabd.org/ongoing_programs.htm; access on 5/11/2018).

Kingshuk Multipurpose Cooperative Society: Community Solutions for Housing Without Subsidy or Finance

In 1987, seven friends began saving US$1 per month; by 1989, 70 other friends had joined in. To commemorate the tragic death of one of their number, they started a book fair, a community library, neighborhood cleaning, and blood donation programs. In 1991, after completing University, the original seven friends formed a Cooperative Society with 121 voting members. The 5000 project members, who had the liberty to withdraw at any time with an assurance of getting a return at a rate higher than the banks, had invested their savings in 270 transport vehicles. In 1994, *Kingshuk*, the Cooperative Society, bought some low-cost land in suburban Dhaka, matching members' savings to build housing on the land and sell it to members (Retrieved from http://72.167.179.155/kingshuk/history.htm; accessed on 23/11/2017).

Coalition for the Urban Poor (CUP): NGOs Work Together for a Common Cause

Coalition for the Urban Poor (CUP) has been working since 1989 for the improvement of the livelihood strategy of the urban poor (Banks 2006). They coordinated their actions to avoid duplication, improve program design and identify the needs of their poor clients. Through an informal group known as BURT, CUP maintained networks with different organizations, including government, nongovernments, and research and educational institutions (BURT 2005). The work of CUP remained concentrated in Dhaka and Chittagong, and part of Khulna.

CUP also acted as a policy advocate in developing national policies to reduce urban poverty. CUP also tried to coordinate the policies of the Government and projects of international donors for the urban poor. One of CUP's main policy issues was eviction. CUP negotiated with Governments to prevent evictions and convinced the caretaker Government of 2007–2009 to restrict evictions and resettle evicted persons.[3] Another CUP issue was voting rights for informal settlement dwellers, which it succeeded in getting in 1994. In 2000, CUP began creating Slum Dwellers' Protection Committees (BOSCs) from these informal settlement dwellers. With 2 million members, Banks (2006) concluded that the establishment of BOSCs had permitted the urban poor to express their difficulties to the representatives of municipal government bodies, on issues such as water supply, sanitation and electricity. Over the years, BOSCs replaced often-violent rallies and demonstrations with effective negotiations with local officials behind closed doors as their major strategy.

CARE-Bangladesh: An International NGO Alleviating Poverty in Bangladesh

As a multinational NGO, CARE implemented a poverty alleviation program titled *Shouhardo* in 16 municipalities of Bangladesh for a period of five years, in partnership with CUP and BURT. With financial assistance from UNICEF and the Government of Bangladesh, CARE-BD completed the implementation of a project entitled "Environmental Sanitation, Hygiene and Water Supply in Urban Slums and Fringes Project" where they worked with around 1 million slum people. The main focus of the project was to ensure land rights for, and the resettlement of, slum people in Jessore and Dinajpur by mobilizing the people living in these slums (CARE-BD 2002). One of the most effective initiatives of CARE and its network partners, including donor agencies, was to hold a dialogue with the Caretaker Government (2007–2008) to stop removal of people living in slums.

LOSAUK: Theatre as Politics

LOSAUK was a development-based research institute in Khulna, created in 1987. Conducting research, building awareness and conducting advocacy and networking were the main functions of this organization. While conducting advocacy on human rights, they preferred the use of tools like theatre. The main focus of their activities was the building of networks

[3] The interim government took the decision on 17 March 2007.

among the adolescent women of slums so that they could carry out advocacy campaigns on their rights, tenancy safety, supply of water and hygienic sanitation. (Retrieved from http://www.losauk.org/details/index.html; accessed on 23/12/2018,)

Concern Bangladesh: Changing Itself First

For 25–30 years, Concern Bangladesh has worked in urban slums, improving conditions and livelihoods for those who lived there. In the new millennium, Concern faced increasing competition in the urban slums from other NGOs. So the organization changed its structure from a "sectoral" to a "contextual" focus. Concern focused on specific groups or areas rather than urban slums in general, working with partners rather than doing its own projects. The group phased out all urban projects by 2006 (Banks 2006).

Conclusion

The above discussion suggests that the issue of slum upgradation has been in progress in Bangladesh since the 1990s, when the country first started to experience unprecedented growth in urbanization and in urban poverty. Thus, the Government, along with different NGOs, has been working on the issue of development of the livelihood of people living in slums through three approaches: slum clearance, slum relocation and slum upgradation. Among these three, the best approach proved to be slum upgradation as the other two options proved problematic both for the State and for the slum dwellers. Among different programs, a number of these have been found to be successful in developing the conditions of slum dwellers in the country. These are Dushtha Shahthya Kendra, implementing "Improving Rights to Services for Slum Dwellers in Dhaka", WaterAid-financed and VERC-implemented "Community-Led Total Sanitation Program (CTLS)", UNICEF-financed and GoB-implemented "Slum Improvement Project (SIP), and CARE, Bangladesh-implemented "Integrated Food Security Program (IFSP)". In addition to these giant projects, there are many projects that are also working for the development of different slums in the country.

Most of the programs that have been a success in improving the situation of slum dwellers in Bangladesh were successful because they encouraged community participation in the implementation process. As a result, people continued to carry out different activities of these projects even after the termination of the projects. The success of some of the projects was limited to the extent that they overlapped with other projects of other agencies, demanded that the poor pay more than they could afford to participate or failed to provide for the hardcore poor who could do little to help themselves. The subsequent chapter draws more-general conclusions.

References

Ahmed, R. (2006). *A case study on reaching the poorest & vulnerable.* Paper presented in 32nd WEDC conference, November, Colombo, Sri Lanka. Retrieved May 23, 2010, from http://www.wateraid.org/documents/plugin_documents/case_study__reaching_the_poorest_and_most_vulnerable__pstc.pdf.

Asian Development Bank. (2009). Community-driven development country profile: Bangladesh. Retrieved June 10, 2010, from http://www.adb.org/Documents/Participation/Country-Brief-Bangladesh.pdf.

Banks, N. (2006). A tale of two wards: Political participation and the urban poor in Dhaka City. *Working Paper.* Center for Governance Studies. Dhaka: BRAC University.

Bold, M. V. d., Uwejamomere, T., & Vandermeer, K. (2010). *Raising visibility and voices of the urban poor: Civil society's engagement in urban water and sanitation reform—Experiences from WaterAid country programs.* A report prepared for WaterAid. Retrieved May 23, 2010, from http://www.wateraid.org/documents/plugin_documents/engaging_with_service_providers_final.pdf.

BURT. (2005). Dialogue with donors on urban poverty issues. Dhaka: CARE, Bangladesh.

CARE, Bangladesh (2002). Integrated Food Security Program (IFSP), Midterm Evaluation Report, Prepared by TANGO International, Inc. in collaboration with Human Development Research Centre, HDRC, Dhaka.

GHK. (2006). *LPUPAP: Report of evaluation mission.* UK: GHK International.

Habib, E. (2009). The role of government and NGOs in slum development: The case of Dhaka City. *Development in Practice, 19*(2), 259–265.

Islam, N. (Ed.). (1997). *Urban research in Bangladesh.* Dhaka: UPL.

Islam, R., Mustafa, S. and Patkar, A. (2006). *Poverty Impact Assessment LPUPAP.* Dhaka, LPUPAP.

Jinnah, S. I. A. (2007). Rights of water connections for urban slum dwellers in Bangladesh: A study on DSK's experience in three slums of Mirpur, Dhaka. Dhaka: WaterAid, Bangladesh. Retrieved June 2, 2010, from http://www.wateraid.org/documents/plugin_documents/water_points_for_urban_slum_dwellers.pdf.

Menon, B. (n.d.). Informal settlement upgrading in Dhaka: Sector study, urban housing and informal settlements in Bangladesh. Washington, DC: World Bank.
Retrieved November 23, 2017, from http://72.167.179.155/kingshuk/history.htm.
Retrieved December 23, 2016, from http://webapps01.un.org/nvp/frontend!policy.action?id=192.
Retrieved December 5, 2017, from http://www.ifpri.org/dataset/bangladesh-2.
Retrieved December 23, 2018, from http://www.losauk.org/details/index.html.
Retrieved December 7, 2018, from http://www.nabolokbd.org/urban.htm.
Retrieved November 5, 2018, from http://www.shevabd.org/ongoing_programs.htm.

CHAPTER 7

Conclusion, Challenges and Recommendations

Conclusion

We have seen from all the preceding chapters that rapid growth of urbanization has indeed become an important feature of developing countries; the United Nations (2014) has also affirmed the same. Almost half the total population (globally) who live in urban areas are actually living in squatter settlements with almost no decent living conditions, as it is not affordable. Of course, the government of developing countries has been failing to provide decent housing to these people (Turok et al. 2017). That is why urban slums have been sprouting up in all major cities of the world, with minimal to no housing, deteriorating living conditions, and the growing perils of climate change along with other exclusionary urban forms (Mathur 2013; Ahmed 2016).

Urbanization today is still not free from poverty; lack of income opportunities is swelling the population of urban slums in most developing countries. We feel that there is an opportunity even in these dark days; urban slums could be developed to generate income opportunities and implement activities relating to human development. Aluko (2011), in a study on cities of Nigeria, mentioned that increasing rate of poverty and urbanization have posed a serious challenge to the dignity, social cohesion and the administrative efficiency of the cities by creating pressure on urban basic services.

Generally, slum development initiatives have been taken thus far, not only to overcome the problem of the slum dwellers' lower/no income,

P. K. Panday, *The Face of Urbanization and Urban Poverty in Bangladesh*, https://doi.org/10.1007/978-981-15-3332-7_7

but also to help them overcome multiple other challenges that they are confronted with. These include land tenure insecurity, poor quality housing, inadequate water supply, and problems of sanitation and drainage. Slum people suffer from Prisoners' Dilemma Condition, that is, they do not demand better or improved housing, as improvement of one house will have no impact on the real estate value of the property. Thus, in order to impact the real estate value, other slum dwellers of the neighborhood would be required to exhibit the same level of demand (Klosterman 1985). Having said that, individual slum dwellers are certainly not barred from affording the cost of improvement of services; however, the likelihood of their success of the individual is very low (Pugh 1996).

Based on extensive literature review and other studies thus far, we feel that improving slums by the government alone is a difficult task to attain. We have also seen different state and nonstate actors who have invested money and effort in this regard. While working from a different perspective, the emphasis was also given on building a network among organizations working in these lines with the assumption that these networks and associations could play a critical role in resolving the Prisoners' Dilemma by developing basic services. Edelman and Mitra (2006) mentioned that the self-sufficiency of slum people living in Delhi for instance, increased greatly through social network. That is why their dependence on political contracts for different types of services also reduced.

The growth of slums has a strong positive relationship with the macroeconomic environment of a country. Thus, the respective governments should make policies aiming to create more income opportunities for slum dwellers, so that they could afford their basic necessities, including housing. Along with government interventions, attention needs to be paid to capacity-building measures of local authorities, so that they reach the last mile, and can undertake different services properly. Importantly, governments should also deal with the issue of land tenure rights of the people living in slums, as it has been seen that different government agencies prepare a plan for using those lands without considering the vulnerabilities of the people living there (UN-HABITAT 2009).

From the analysis of different chapters, it has been learnt that incidence of the growth of slums is quite high in those countries that have been experiencing a high rate of urbanization. This has compelled governments to think about sustainable urbanization. This requires meticulous implementation planning by the governments, whereby they could address problems of informal settlements, while keeping provisions of better infrastructure along with other essential services like water, sanitation, garbage collection, drains, street lights, among others (UN-HABITAT 2009).

Therefore, if we really want to upgrade the situation of people living in the slums, we should consider the possible relationship between poverty, slums and sustainable development. We have already argued that poverty is one of the root causes of migration of people in cities, which is ultimately responsible for slum formation. Thus, in order to solve the issue relating to slums, we should identify strategies through which a sustainable solution could be reached to end this burning crisis. Poverty does have different dimensions in different countries, as the context is not the same. Thus, when it concerns the issue of slum upgradation, the poverty situation of particular slums needs to be considered with greater emphasis. Different initiatives have been taken so far in different parts of the world by governments, international organizations, national and international NGOs. Every organization has used a particular strategy to deal with the issue of slum upgradation. However, there are some initiatives that have been considered as the best practice due to their successful implementation. Notably, most of the slum-upgrading success stories have used community development approach in their program in order to create a sense of ownership among the slum people, so that they could carry forward the same initiatives after the project is officially phased out. This has helped in attaining sustainability of the project.

The following are some slum-upgrading success stories through programs like Calcutta's "Basti Improvement Program" (BIP) and "Bharavi" in Mumbai in India, Comprehensive Kampung Improvement Program in Surabaya, Indonesia C-KIP Community Participation Model in Thailand, Baan Mankong: Secure Housing in Thailand, Kenya's Community Federation and City Upgradation: The Work of Pamoja Trust and Muungano, Slum Development program in Manila, Philippines, and Twin Track Approach. All of them have been established as measures/benchmarks of best practices.

Influenced by some of the global best practices, different organizations have implemented several slum-upgrading initiatives in different parts of the country. Among the different programs, a number of programs have outscored others by attaining enormous success. These programs include DSK's implementation of "Improving Rights to Services for Slum Dwellers in Dhaka", WaterAid financed and VERC implemented "Community-Led Total Sanitation Program" (CTLS), UNICEF financed and GoB implemented "Slum Improvement Project" (SIP), and CARE, Bangladesh implemented "the Integrated Food Security Program (IFSP)". In addition to these projects, other projects have also attained a great amount of success. In most of the cases, these projects have stressed the importance of community participation in the project implementation with the expectation that they would consider the project as their own initiative.

Nevertheless, a pertinent question arises: what lessons may be learnt from slum-upgrading best practices in Bangladesh, for instance, and across the world. To be more specific, what learning could be considered worthy during the design of new slum-upgrading initiatives? The lessons could be considered important for the government and national and international organizations who aspire to carry out slum-upgrading initiatives.

First: Focus On People Not Infrastructure

Seeing a tatty place where people are living in misery, without basic amenities, evokes a natural reaction to tear it all down and rebuild it in sparkling condition; yet this is the worst practice. Unless you can organize and empower the people, train and give them control of their own lives and communities, the infrastructure you create will quickly decay, and the lives of the people would not change. Thus, one must look to organize the people into community-based organizations, train them, supply resources or, better, give the people ideas about how to create their own resources, like cooperative societies and negotiating with banks, landlords and local governments, if necessary, even act as a guarantor. It is only then that the people having the power, ownership in their hands, would look to build and maintain the infrastructure that they need.

Second: People Need Partners Not Prima Donnas

The most effective projects have been those that have united community-based organizations, individual poor people and families, NGOs, local governments, the private sector and the State sector to work together on specific "do-able" changes, not those done only by the government or only by one NGO.

Third: Innovation, Not Infrastructure

New ideas, like LOSAUK, CUP, Kingshuk, SHEVA, etc., have had a surprising impact in getting others to act and making change happen. There is more to social change than sticking bricks together.

Fourth: Act Short-Term But Think Long-Term

One of the major problems with international donor or bank funds, or NGO projects, is that they are temporary. The average project seems to last about 5 years. When NGOs try to extend their action in the long term, like "Concern Bangladesh", they may overstretch themselves, and in the process, collapse. Yet, the successful projects were those that addressed issues of sustainability and building structures at the community level, which could continue the progress of the project even after the interveners had long gone. The last thing the poor need is "flash in the pan" solutions. After you are a memory, they still have to live there.

Major Challenges to Slum Upgrading in Bangladesh

Dealing with people living in slums where they do not have any land rights or access to better amenities like drinking water, sanitation, electricity, better drainage facilities, health, and so on is quite difficult. Whoever has begun implementation of slum-upgrading initiatives must have considered these realities before they commenced their initiatives. Although many initiatives have attained success in terms of improving the living conditions of the distressed people of slums, they have faced different obstacles during the implementation of the projects. The following obstacles have hindered the process of implementation of their programs.

First: The first problem is that all the basic utility services (i.e. infrastructure, water supply) to the slums are provided by the government. Thus, the government does not show much interest in investing money for infrastructure development in the slums, since such infrastructure development may offer permanence to these slums. On the other hand, NGOs usually carry out programs on sanitation, offer tube wells and provide micro-credits for the well-being of the people living in slums. Different organizations carry out different programs without consulting each other. Thus, there is an urgent need for coordination among different service providers.

Second: A very few organizations including the government carry out programs on housing for slum-dwellers. Due to strict government regulations, and control on urban land along with its distribution, NGOs do not show enthusiasm to work for better housing for the people living in slums. Sivam (2003) identified four constraints for public formal and informal housing development in developing countries. These are: (i) existing tenuous policies, regulations and controls; (ii) poor coordination and management among public agencies; (iii) lack of reasonable loan facilities for middle and lower-income groups; (iv) the absence of sound housing delivery system. On the other hand, a study conducted by Islam (2000) found that 20% of Dhaka's residential land is actually occupied by the poor; and among them, 97% do not have land ownership (cited in Rahman et al. 2005). Thus, NGOs feel reluctant to carry out programs on housing ahead of savings and credit, which compel the slum dwellers in turn to arrange their own housing. In most cases, slum dwellers live in houses that are found to be unhealthy, and at times even lack proper ventilation.

Third: Many NGOs and international organizations do not show enough interest in intervening in the slums for fear of government evictions. There are several instances where the government evicted several slums from different places. Even different NGOs went to Court against the decision of the government for eviction (Lankatilleke 2002; Habib 2009). In some cases, the High Court issued directions for the government not to evict people living in the slums without making any alternative arrangements to settle them (Habib 2009). Thus, different NGOs lose their interest to invest in the slums where there is a lot of uncertainty.

Fourth: The government of Bangladesh considers slums a liability and does not show sufficient enthusiasm to build long-term strategic plans for slum upgradation. At times, sporadic initiatives are indeed undertaken; however, they fail to leave any positive impact on the overall upgradation of the slums.

Fifth: Since there are thousands of slums in Dhaka city, and given that Dhaka is the national the capital, most of the organizations that carry out intervention programs in slums, devote their attention to Dhaka-based slums. As a result, slums of other parts of the country do not get adequate attention.

Sixth: Most of the NGOs are foreign-funded. Thus, they are driven more by the ideologies of their donors while choosing the priority areas for the programs instead of considering the real needs of the urban population living in the slums. In such a situation, the programs do not reflect the real needs of the slum dwellers.

Finally, there is hardly any coordination among different organizations working for slum-upgradation programs. Each organization seems to be carrying out their programs differently. Thus it is seen that different organizations are carrying out their intervention programs on the same slum, which deprive other slums from availing of the facilities provided by NGOs. If slums intervention guidelines were in place, it could be possible to coordinate these activities.

Overcoming the Problems of Slum: What is the Way Out?

In the context of Bangladesh, the adaptation of slum clearance and slum relocation approach is not possible. For instance, if we talk about Dhaka city, it is neither possible to clear almost 5000 slums (as has been indicated by some NGOs), nor is it possible to relocate these slums outside of Dhaka, since it is very difficult to find places adjacent to Dhaka for relocation. Thus, the only way that could help reduce the intensity of problems relating to slum dwellers is slum-upgradation programs. Of course, it is very difficult for the government to bear all responsibilities of slum upgradation alone. NGOs should and could play an important role here; in fact, some NGOs have carried out various slum-upgradation programs. The following suggestions could be taken into consideration in overcoming the problems of slum dwellers.

First: There is hardly any official statistics regarding the total number of slums in Bangladesh. Different organizations have put forward their statistics, which differ to a large extent. Thus, the government should first pay attention to the issue of identifying the total number of slums in Bangladesh. If there is a complete statistic, it would help the government to design its slum-upgradation programs methodically.

Second: Very often it is seen in Bangladesh that the process of policy-making and implementation suffers from lack of coordination among different actors. In the context of slum-upgradation programs, since the government, NGOs and different international organizations are working on the issue separately, it is necessary that these diverse efforts must be well-coordinated, so that the actual problems of the slum dwellers could be addressed.

Third: Slum dwellers should be considered as important stakeholders in this process of upgradation; they shouldn't be identified as a burden for the government. Efforts should be made on identifying areas where intervention is necessary. This could be done through extensive research carried out by experienced professionals in this field. After identifying important areas, interventions should be made through government–NGO collaboration.

Fourth: Providing housing to the people living in slums is a matter of great importance. In a country like Bangladesh, providing housing to slum dwellers through the government is almost impossible, since a project of this size and scale requires considerable funds, and cannot be dependent on the government alone. NGOs therefore need to step up. The government could provide a congenial environment for the NGOs by easing rules and regulations so that they could work efficiently (Rahman 2005; Habib 2009). Apart from enabling a congenial working environment for NGOs in the housing sector, the government could also make an allotment in the national budget for building low-rent flats for slum dwellers. For instance, the government could take a lesson from the Baan Mankong: Secure Housing in Thailand and Dharavi of India. These two cases are regarded as the best practices of providing housing to the urban poor.

Although the government of Bangladesh is considering building high-rise low-rent flats for the middle-class residents of Dhaka city, people living in the slums would not be able to avail this opportunity since they will be required to pay an amount for each flat. Moreover, given the huge number of slum dwellers in Dhaka city, it would not be possible for the government to build the required number of flats in the city.

Fifth: Availing of water supply is a fundamental opportunity for every citizen. It is no exception for the people living in slums. In Bangladesh, there is a legal proviso when issuing permission to provide water supply to a household. The legal binding is that every household should have land ownership to obtain water supply. Thus, slum dwellers are not entitled to avail the opportunity of water supply legally since they do not have legal land entitlements. In this regard, the contribution of Dushtha Shaystha Kendra (DSK) Bangladesh is worth acknowledging. As a result of DSK's intermediary role, DWASA has taken the decision to offer water supply in the slum through Community-Based Organizations. Thus, the government should provide directions to these authorities (water supply authorities) throughout Bangladesh so that people living in slums may avail water supply facility.

Sixth: Different NGOs through providing training and technical support are trying to make slum dwellers aware of different aspects of their lives. Without the awareness, slum-upgradation programs would not be successful, since they are the main stakeholders. Thus, the government should encourage these NGOs to initiate more programs. Mumtaz (2001) in this regard stated that the government should not offer penalties to different NGOs; instead they should use the power to motivate them. Being motivated by the government, if NGOs carry out more capacity-building programs in the slums, then the community will be able to manage their own problems, which ultimately would help in upgrading the situation of the slum.

Seventh: Successful policy implementation requires active participation of different stakeholders in the policy-making and implementation process. Thus, all slum-upgrading programs should be designed in such a way that the stakeholders may take part in designing the program and its implementation. Only then will a sense of ownership develop among the community members, who in turn would help the program achieve success.

Finally: In the context of Bangladesh, eradication of slums is not possible. Once slum dwellers of a particular place are evicted, they would gather in other places, which would establish a new slum. Thus, slum upgradation is the only solution to this problem, and the only way forward.

References

Ahmed, I. (2016). Building resilience of urban slums in Dhaka, Bangladesh. *Procedia—Social and Behavioral Sciences, 218*, 202–213.

Aluko, O. E. (2011). Sustainable housing, population growth and poverty: The implications on Lagos Mega City. *Journal of Sustainable Development, 4*(4), 138–144.

Edelman, B., & Mitra, A. (2006). Slum-dwellers' access to basic amenities: The role of political contact, its determinants and adverse effects. *Review of Urban and Regional Development Studies, 18*(1), 25–40.

Habib, E. (2009). The role of government and NGOs in slum development: The case of Dhaka City. *Development in Practice, 19*(2), 259–265.

Islam K. N. (2000). Temporal mapping and spatial analysis of land transformation due to urbanization and its import on surface water system: A case from Dhaka

metropolitan area. *International Archives of the Photogrammetry, Remote Sensing, XXX*(B7): Amsterdam.
Klosterman, R. E. (1985). Arguments for and against planning. *The Town Planning Review, 56*(1), 5–20.
Lankatilleke, L. (2002). Urban cleansing in Dhaka. *Urban Poor Asia Journal.* Retrieved March 10, 2013, from http://www.achr.net/new_page_10.htm.
Mathur, O. P. (2013). *Urban poverty in Asia.* Manila: Asian Development Bank. Retrieved October 12, 2017, from https://www.adb.org/sites/default/files/project-document/81002/urban-povertyasia.pdf.
Mumtaz, B. (2001). Why cities need slums. *Habitat Debate, 7*(3), 20–21.
Pugh, C. (1996). *Sustainability, the environment and urbanisation.* London: Earthscan.
Rahman, M. R., Islam, A. H. M., & Hassan, M. S. (2005). Change detection of winter crop coverage and the use of Landsat data with GIS. *J. Geo-Environ., 4*: 1–13.
Sivam, A. (2003). Viewpoint: Housing supply in Delhi. *Cities, 20*(2), 135–141.
Turok, I., Budlender, J., & Visagie, J. (2017). The role of informal urban settlements in upward mobility. *Development Policy Research Unit Working Paper 201505.* DPRU, University of Cape Town.
UN-HABITAT. (2009). *Planning sustainable cities: Global report on human settlements 2009.* London: Earthscan.
United Nations. (2014). *World urbanization prospects: The 2014 revision.* Washington, DC: Population Division of UN DESA.

Index[1]

[1] Note: Page numbers followed by 'n' refer to notes.

P. K. Panday, *The Face of Urbanization and Urban Poverty in Bangladesh*, https://doi.org/10.1007/978-981-15-3332-7

The manufacturer's authorised representative in the EU is Springer Nature Customer Service Centre GmbH, Europaplatz 3, 69115 Heidelberg, Germany. If you have any concerns regarding our products, please contact ProductSafety@springernature.com

Printed and bound by CPI Group (UK) Ltd, Croydon, CR0 4YY
25/09/2026
02222902-0014